ANGLICAN ATTITUDES

A Study of
Victorian Religious Controversies

BY

A. O. J. COCKSHUT

COLLINS
ST. JAMES'S PLACE, LONDON
1959

ANGLICAN ATTITUDES

A Study of
Victorian Religious Controversies

By the Same Author
ANTHONY TROLLOPE

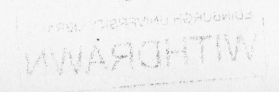

To Gill

ACKNOWLEDGMENT

I am most grateful to Mr. R. A. Denniston for his valuable help in the choice and arrangement of facts and ideas for this book.

A. O. J. C

Contents

Preface

It seems to me that the quarter of a century which followed Newman's reception into the Roman Church in 1845, is a period of exceptional importance in the history of the Church of England. For almost at the same time three things happened. The threat from Rome, for so long felt to be merely political, emerged as an intellectual and moral one. The threat of agnosticism became, for the first time, too obvious and coherent to be ignored even by the most unobservant churchman (and for this reason I have included a chapter on Victorian agnosticism). And the Church of England lost its previous comfortable position as the one respectable, politically dominant creed with a virtual monopoly of higher education and intellectual life.

Every reader of Newman's ' *Apologia* ' will have been struck by the extraordinarily Anglican nature of the experience and argument which ultimately led him away from the Church of England. With perhaps the solitary exception of Wiseman's article on the Donatists, there were *no* contemporary Roman Catholic influences, personal or literary, upon Newman between 1833 and 1845. The men who influenced him had been dead for fifteen centuries. This indicates the strength of the Anglican intellectual monopoly, which was fostered, of course, by the requirement that undergraduates should subscribe the Articles. But this monopoly was coming to an end more rapidly than anyone could guess. The way the Church reacted to the change makes a fascinating study. And these twenty-five years of crisis produced many surprising revelations about the Church of England.

In choosing for detailed consideration three Anglican controversies and passing over others equally celebrated, I have had several considerations in mind. It seems to me that the Gorham case, *Essays and Reviews* and the Colenso case fulfil all the following conditions: they were celebrated in their time and attracted comment from some of the most distinguished minds of the period: they dealt with issues of permanent religious interest: they illustrated divergent possibilities, often generally unnoticed before, in the original Anglican formulas of the sixteenth century: and they illustrated the practical working of a religious system in which the ultimate decision is claimed by the secular power.

CHAPTER ONE

Introductory

IT HAS long been customary to think of the intellectual and
spiritual history of the Victorian period in terms of orthodoxy and revolt. Orthodoxy is often thought of as the solid,
inherited doctrines of ecclesiastical authorities, supported
by the powerful and respectable; and the rebel whether
Darwin or Newman, Maurice or Colenso, is fighting a
battle with few friends against great odds. But it seems to
me that the three *causes célèbres* with which this book deals
present a very different picture. Ecclesiastical authority
not only acted for a long time diffidently and inconsistently,
but was regularly in conflict with the authority of the State;
while the various organs of the State's authority were
frequently at odds among themselves. Apparently lonely
rebels often commanded wide support, popular, respectable,
and even official. And by 1870 it would hardly be an
exaggeration to say that it was the agnostics rather than the
orthodox who had the sense of being official, an intellectual
establishment more powerful than the church establishment.

In 1855, for instance, the following lines were written
about F. D. Maurice, a theological rebel whose orthodoxy
and honesty had both been impugned, and whose academic
position was threatened:

> *For, being of the honest few,*
> *Who give the Fiend himself his due,*

11

Should eighty-thousand college-councils
Thunder anathema, friend, at you;
Should all our churchmen foam in spite
At you, so careful of the right
Yet one lay-hearth would give you welcome.

Who wrote this? Not Swinburne but Tennyson, Poet
Laureate, beloved of Queen Victoria. A man who had
received such an imprimatur could not really be lonely.
In his distrust of ecclesiastical authority, as in so many other
ways, Tennyson perfectly expressed the views of a vast, and
perhaps a dominant concensus of educated and respectable
opinion.

There is no doubt that injustices were done to indivi-
duals who were wrongly supposed to have contravened the
Anglican formularies. But this was largely because the
ecclesiastical authorities were often in a nervous, even
panicky state. If one wants a serene and confident statement of doctrine, by a man certain that his opponents are
in retreat, one does not go to Archbishops Longley or Tait,
but to an agnostic like George Eliot or T. H. Huxley, or a
Roman Catholic like Newman or an Anglican rebel like
Jowett or Colenso.

There were a number of reasons why Anglican ecclesiastical authority should operate in an indecisive way in the
1840's and 1850's. One has the feeling, in reading books
written before 1800, in Boswell's life of Johnson, for instance,
that the arguments against Christianity and against the
Church of England are known, and that there is a recognised answer to each. In the 1840's and after this is not so.
The attack could come from so many different quarters at
once. Biblical criticism from Germany and evolutionary
ideas later codified by Darwin combined to throw doubt on
the Bible, hitherto the foundation both of Anglican and

Protestant doctrines. On the other hand there was the Oxford Movement, which brought insistently before the public the whole thorny question: "Is the Church of England Catholic or Protestant, or a mixture of the two?" And, following from this, the equally difficult question, "If it is a mixture, who is to determine the proportions of the mixture?" Deep and widespread uncertainty on fundamental points like this perhaps helps to explain the extraordinary public reaction to the Tractarians. Newman, Keble and the rest were men who aimed to *preserve*. They believed that the creeds recognised by the Church of England were true. They had no wish, at any rate in the 1830's, the early days of the Movement, to be innovators. The experimental side of twentieth century Anglo-Catholicism, and some later Victorian 'Puseyism', represented by ritualism, daring theological speculation and extreme views on social questions was alien to them. The enemy they set out to attack was what they called liberalism—a term, of course, used in a specialised sense without political connotations. By liberalism they meant the idea that everyone ought to adopt the religious principles which best suited his instincts and temperament, regardless of their claim to objective truth. They believed in the Church of England as part of the world-wide Catholic Church. They believed in the creeds, in the Bible, and above all, they believed in the sacred office and authority of the English bishops, though they had reasonably enough certain reservations about their personality, intellect and courage. Their great aim can be summed up thus: they wanted to remind the clergy and laity of England that the words they recited each week in the creed really meant something.

Yet this modest-seeming programme met with implacable and sometimes frenzied hostility from ecclesiastical authority and from large sections of lay opinion. Now, of course, opposition from Evangelicals was to be expected. They had a different view of the Church's nature, a different conception of dogma, and they could not be expected to agree with Keble and Newman. Opposition from agnostics was also natural. But the most vehement, and incomparably the most puzzling, opposition came from neither of these two groups, but from Anglicans, who saw in the Tractarian movement, not a fight to re-establish Anglican principles, but something new, incomprehensible and perilous. To such people even to mention the words " Holy Catholic Church " (except of course when reciting them in Church) seemed an act of subversion if not indeed of obscenity.

These unreflective Anglicans no doubt dimly felt that ' The Holy Catholic Church is the Church of England as by law established '. But the Tractarians, of course, taking the idea of a Catholic Church seriously, regarded it as quite distinct from the establishment, which was a mere arrangement of human convenience. Therefore they would have been prepared, in certain circumstances, though generally with great regret, to forgo the establishment and defy the State, where matters of religious principle were involved. It was this willingness to sacrifice material interests and privileges which made them so unpopular with some churchmen. There were not a few who felt that the Reform Bill of 1832 was a herald of doom. And there were people, ostensibly supporting the Church who were enemies of its privileges at a time when it had plenty of enemies outside its boundaries. It is easy to see that, in these circumstances, the idea might grow up in excited minds that the Tractarians were traitors. Opponents of this type, unlike Evangelical or agnostic opponents, revealed themselves as men who had not really thought out their own position. Often this was not due to stupidity or laziness, but to a conviction that custom and loyalty were better guides than reason, and that it would be dangerous to enquire deeply into first principles. It is easy to imagine how perturbed such people would be when the restlessly ratiocinative W. G. Ward proclaimed that as a matter of pure reason he could believe the whole of Roman doctrine, and still honestly sign the Thirty-Nine Articles. If the Articles could be made to mean that, they might just as well mean anything else that anyone chose to make them mean.

As time went on, these ambiguous Anglican formulas were less and less able to cover the vast area of controversy or to provide a firm decision between conflicting views. In 1850, Gorham, Phillpotts, his bishop and Gladstone were all arguing expertly about baptismal regeneration, and all appealed to the formulas to vindicate them. And Gorham and Phillpotts met and argued in one room. By comparison with the controversies which followed this one presented relatively manageable issues. But even so, it proved indecisive, and the formulas were not found sufficiently clear to decide it. But by the sixties Bishop Colenso and his metropolitan, Gray, were propounding two totally different theories of religion, and no formula could possible decide the issue. They were not arguing about the same subject. It was at this point that the English bishops in a body came to the conclusion that the sixteenth century formulas and the Victorian secular courts had shown themselves incapable of deciding questions of doctrine and loyalty. And they decided they must ignore the law and fill the vacuum by the exercise of a corporate spiritual authority whose very existence was, of course, in dispute in their own Church. There were several features of the Church of England which made it difficult for authority to be effectively asserted. In the first place, it was generally held to be a Protestant church. Most normal, respectable people (like Queen Victoria, for instance) took it for granted that this was so. And they were not in the least impressed by anyone who pointed out that the word Protestant does not occur in the Prayer Book, while belief in the holy Catholic Church is an article of the creed. Protestantism meant to many people the idea that private judgment was a safer guide to true doctrine than any religious authority. There was a widespread feeling that it would have been a waste of time to cast off the authority of Rome as the " heroes of the Reformation " had done merely to set up another ecclesiastical authority. The very idea of a Protestant authority seemed to many like a monstrous paradox. And we shall see that when Colenso, a man of sensitive conscience and honour, was taunted with retaining Anglican preferment when he had abandoned Anglican doctrine, he had no hesitation in justifying his conduct by comparing himself to Wycliffe and Cranmer who "did not resign as soon as they became Protestant". Whatever view of the Reformation one might think proper for Anglicans, it was hard to deny that it was a considerable upheaval; and men like Colenso argued that Anglicans, having based their structure upon one such upheaval, had no logical right to declare *a priori* that there ought never to be another.

Then it was easy enough to talk about Church authority, but just where did that authority lie? There was a perpetual tension between the Catholic (and Anglican) idea of Church government by bishops, the Protestant (and Anglican) idea of the supremacy of private judgment, and the peculiarly Anglican idea of Church Government by kings. As we shall see there were grave difficulties in the way of a consistent decision from either bishops or the law courts representing the Crown.

First, and most obviously, the bishops did not agree among themselves. In the Gorham case, for instance, Phillpotts, Bishop of Exeter, believed in baptismal regenera-

tion; Gorham, one of his clergy, did not. So throughout
the case, Phillpotts seemed to represent authority, firm and
dutiful, or interfering and tyrannical, according to the point
of view. Gorham's party seemed to represent private
judgment, courageous and conscientious or heretical and
rebellious according to the point of view. But it could so
easily have been the other way round. There were bishops,
of whom the Archbishop of York was one, who agreed with
Gorham. There were inferior clergy living under the
jurisdiction of such bishops, who agreed with Phillpotts. It
was a geographical accident which decided which theological
view was to wear the garb of authority. The point was neatly
illustrated when Bishop Phillpotts, having pronounced
excommunication, as it were, downwards upon Gorham,
was eventually forced by the logic of his position to pronounce it upwards upon the Archbishop of Canterbury.
And geography was to assume an even greater importance
some years later, in the Colenso case. The agnostics,
recognising no authority of this local kind, but looking, for
the most part, to a generally agreed body of principles,
tended to be much more united.

Perhaps the most serious handicap to any decisive action
of ecclesiastical authority arose from the nature of the
Prayer Book and the Thirty-Nine Articles. These were the
only standard of Anglican doctrine recognised by the law of
England; and judges could apply no other test. But it had
become clear in the 1840's when Ward made the remark
already quoted, and Newman rubbed home the point
ingeniously in Tract XC that a clever man could make the
Articles mean pretty well what he liked. Thus the judges
began the hearing of each ecclesiastical case knowing they
were bound to use criteria which had already proved
inadequate to the purpose of judging and distinguishing
doctrines. Some people were quick to realise that if they

could mean so much more than their general drift suggested, they might also mean much less. And in 1860, one of contributors to *Essays and Reviews* held that honest the subscription to the Articles did not commit a man to any religious doctrine whatever.

The fact was, of course, that there was an anomaly in the whole idea of using the Articles as a legal standard. For the Articles clearly assumed that in a Church threatened by doctrinal divisions vagueness and compromise might be helpful. But in law an indeterminate meaning is no meaning at all. *Lex dubia non obligat* is no more than elementary justice. And people who (it was generally felt) were by any standard disloyal to the Church of England could fairly claim that the interpretation they chose to place upon the Articles had equal authority with any other.

There was also a difficulty of a more theoretical nature in using the Articles as a test of orthodoxy. The Articles did not claim to be infallible; they pointed towards scripture as the true rule of faith. But how was it possible for lawyers and judges to follow this pointing? The Bible was obviously a very difficult book and arguments about it had raged for centuries. Every Church and every party in the Church of England claimed it. It was impracticable for a judge to try to settle these venerable controversies about the meaning of the Bible. He could only stick to the Articles, as the law directed, but he might well feel that, in doing so, he was going against the very spirit and intention of the Articles themselves.

Nor did the conscientious judge's difficulties end there. He might well be inclined to ask himself "Why is this man and not someone else on trial before me?" For it was suggested, and probably with truth, that even the most loyal, even the most unadventurous clergyman was nearly always breaking the law. If doctrinal tests were vague the liturgical duties of the clergy were strict. But their strictness was widely felt to be a dead-letter. In practice almost unlimited deviations were permitted, so long as they were Protestant deviations. The Protestant clergyman who complained that his Tractarian neighbour broke the law by saying mass, had generally been breaking it himself all his life (for instance by not publicly reciting the Athanasian creed) and might very well be unaware of the fact.

If the liturgical practice of men esteemed as perfectly loyal Anglicans were in fact illegal, and if manifestly subversive writings did not (in the judgment of lawyers) certainly contravene the Articles then the whole process of testing Anglican loyalty by law was thrown into disrepute.

But the worst difficulty of all for judges lay in the fact that the Articles were written in the sixteenth century. Take, for instance, the vexed question of the authority of Scripture. The Articles concentrated on the question, crucial for Christians of that time, "What is the authority of Scripture, in relation to the authority of the Church and of private judgment?" Biblical inspiration, being generally believed, was taken for granted. In the nineteenth century the situation was very different. The question raised by German criticism, and other current speculations, was " Is the Bible true, in what sense is it true, and how can we know whether it is true? " On this question the Articles were virtually silent. So when several of the contributors to *Essays and Reviews* implied that much of the Bible was only a barbarous farrago of legends, the courts had no legal standards by which to judge their orthodoxy.

It is not surprising then that the operation of the law was uncertain and contradictory. Many earnest spirits, both Anglo-Catholic and Evangelical, felt that it was an intolerable affront both to the Church and to the Christian liberty of the individual to have momentous theological questions decided by secular courts. And they were able to make out a strong case for believing that Erastianism, or complete subordination of Church to State, only hindered the practice of religion. But the practical consequences of State interference were never so bad as they feared. For with such uncertain lights to guide them, judges naturally disagreed, decisions were regularly reversed on appeal, and when the final judgment came, it was not rigorously enforced. No one called in the police to eject heretical incumbents or imprison defiant bishops. The losing party always remained in being as part of the Church of England. No decision of bishops or secular courts was ever decisive. Each decision tended in the end, however lucid it might be in itself, to increase the general confusion because of its disagreement with other decisions. In legal theory there was a known hierarchy of civil courts; in ecclesiastical theory there was a hierarchy of bishops. But in practice there was no final judgment, no recognised end to any controversy, because there was no authority generally accepted by Anglicans as final. Every indecisive decision tended to increase, in the more thoughtful agnostics, their sense of having an intellectual cohesion greater than that of Christians, and to make them more confident of ultimate triumph.

To-day of course, some people will argue that the practical ineffectiveness of both legal and ecclesiastical decisions tended on the whole towards a smooth working of an English system of compromise. Was not the ineffectiveness, in a way, a guarantee of liberty? A fair degree of practical liberty there certainly was. But the picture which the controversies present to us is not exactly one of compromise, but of a series of unmodified opinions, each presented as having authority. Compromises are made in the interests of the practical working of affairs. Here there was no compromise, and affairs did not work. The machinery of ecclesiastical government really came to a standstill.

Englishmen, as we know, respect law; and the utter practical ineffectiveness of the courts in these matters is very striking. They decided with full legal panoply, and their decisions were disregarded. It would seem that a conclusion of both theoretical and practical importance can be drawn from these surprising facts. It is this: State control of religion can only be effective if the State is prepared to persecute. (Whether it will ultimately be effective then is, of course, a separate question with which I do not deal.) The Victorian State, though it could be severe upon minorities, was not prepared to embark on a policy of persecution. The idea of the State sitting in judgment on religion, and appealing not to power, but to justice, ends only in frustration. Judges and politicians, in so far as they act simply as judges and politicians, have not the data to decide religious questions. And if they judge by a legalistic interpretation of religious formulas, as the Victorian judges usually did, all will end in confusion. If, on the other hand, they judge not as judges and politicians, but as amateur theologians, or secular prelates, they will be, and will be felt to be, tyrannical. The only sanction for their decisions then will be physical force. These conclusions, which seem to me to be fully borne out by the history of the three cases which follow, cast a somewhat surprising light upon the whole question of Church establishment and parliamentary control of religion.

It is in its effect on the agnostics that the paradoxical consequences of Church establishment are most obvious. The most striking thing about most leading agnostics of the time (there are notable exceptions, like Clough) is their sense of certainty, of cohesion among themselves, and of comparative freedom from outside interference. Sometimes, it is true, agnostics like Leslie Stephen had to give up university appointments because of their religious opinions. But outside a few clerical preserves, agnostics were free; and even the universities, they believed (correctly as it proved), would soon be fully opened to them. They began to feel more and more that they were semi-official, and that the legal concept of England as a Christian country was becoming a dead-letter. But the harassed clergyman accused of heresy in the Queen's courts, or the much-tried bishop thwarted at every turn by the State in the exercise of his normal authority could not feel that the establishment was a dead-letter. He may often have been inclined to wish that it was. The effect of England's theoretical position as a Christian State was that in religious matters the State always interfered with Christians, and mainly with Christians of the established Church.

The agnostics seemed to have excellent grounds for confidence. But we shall find that in some ways they over-estimated both their practical prospects and the lasting firmness of their intellectual assumptions. At the same time, the Christians on the whole overestimated the lasting importance of their manifold difficulties. One feels inclined, after reading the documents of Victorian religious contro-versy, to enunciate, the dull but (if true) important law: no religious crisis is as damaging to the Christian faith as it seems at the time.

CHAPTER TWO

Doctrine and Authority:
The Agnostic Version

THE GREAT and difficult problems raised by the controversies of the 1850's and 1860's were, of course, in one
sense perennial. At any time since the sixteenth century
Anglicans might be impelled to ask themselves about the
relative authority of the bishops and the Bible, about the
nature of the Royal supremacy, or about the interpretation
of the Articles. But it is impossible to doubt that in the
Victorian period questions such as these acquired a new
urgency and were disputed before a much wider and more
intent audience than ever before. We shall not be able to
understand the magnitude of the change unless we set the
eternal problems of religion against their new Victorian
background—the new agnosticism.

The nineteenth century was the first in which a high
proportion of thinking people in England consciously and
deliberately rejected Christianity. So it is natural that we
should think of Victorian agnostics as rebels. We are apt
to forget how quickly a new movement can acquire settled
habits and a conservative spirit, and even invent for itself
roots in an alien past. Most Victorian agnostics held two
convictions very strongly. One was that religion, in the
sense of doctrine and worship, was rapidly and inevitably
dying; and the other was that the Christian religion,

especially in its Protestant version, contained a vital core of moral truth, which Christians themselves had always under-valued or even ignored, and which the agnostics of the nine-teenth century had first separated out from its debilitating husk of dogma and miracle.

To worried Anglicans, a little puzzled about the precise intellectual basis of their Church's faith, the great agnostic thinkers, Huxley, Spencer, Mill, George Eliot and the rest seemed much more formidable than mere scoffers and sceptics. They believed that they understood the inner meaning of Christ's teaching while His professed followers were committed to a mean, external and untenable view of it. They were immensely confident. They felt sure that the old kind of religion would disappear whether they attacked it or not, and some of them, like George Eliot, were much more afraid that the inner core of moral truth would be trampled down in the stampede away from religion than that an obviously doomed theological system would linger on too long.

It was frightening to Christians, and especially to Angli-cans, who had so recently had almost a monopoly of English intellectual life, and were most severely troubled by feuds among themselves, to see how quickly the agnostic party could cease to be despised outcasts, and become almost official. John Stuart Mill, for instance, had been warned by his agnostic and Benthamite father of the great danger of confessing in public that he had no religious belief. The elder Mill was no coward, but he was giving what seemed in 1830 the only possible prudent advice. In 1877 W. K. Clifford, not an agnostic so much as a militant atheist, felt quite safe in despising German and other continental Catholics for being at odds with their governments. He could regard the religious basis of the British State, the Establishment and the Coronation, as a mere relic, recognised to be such even by those who still believed. In 1892, George Gissing's novel *Born in Exile*, whose story is placed in the 1870's, reveals a self-confidence in unbelievers which is equally startling to contemporary Christian and contemporary agnostic. For we have come to expect that a serious agnostic writer will pay intellectual respect to distinguished believers just as Christian writers will show the same respect to distinguished agnostics. But in Gissing's book the fact that a man has studied geology and yet remains a Christian is treated as incontrovertible proof of his feeble intelligence. When the hero becomes a clergyman, his friends, just because they believe him to be intelligent, take it for granted that he is being hypocritical and accepting for the sake of social advancement a faith which he really regards as foolish. They have no evidence, they simply regard it as certain and obvious that no one with any brain is a Christian nowadays. Gissing was no visionary prophet of atheism; he was a careful and unimaginative recorder of his times, and the calm, unexcited way in which he presents this extraordinary idea as if it were a platitude is most significant.

A whole mass of evidence could be adduced to show how credulous leading agnostics became in their acceptance of anything which combined a refutation of Christianity with an earnest, moral vision. One need perhaps only mention the extraordinary vogue enjoyed by Auguste Comte, whose naïve humane religious seriousness exactly filled the bill. A man who felt able to prophesy the precise changes which must inevitably occur in the frontiers of Europe, who could state without offering evidence that " the education of the individual necessarily follows the same course as the evolution of the race " was revered by such highly intelligent people as George Eliot and John Stuart Mill. Christians have always had to face atheistic scoffers and had no need in the nineteenth century or at any other time to be unduly disturbed by them. But this new attempt to harness the highest religious and moral sensibility to a secular creed was distinctly ominous. It meant that people of very strong religious instincts and a high sense of duty might reject Christianity as having too little of the true religious spirit. George Eliot, for instance, translated that seminal work of destructive Biblical criticism, the *Leben Jesu* of Strauss; and there can be no doubt that the appearance of such works in English influenced many thoughtful people towards the rejection of Christianity. But she went about her work in the most reverent and pious spirit. Her friend Mrs. Bray recorded in a letter of 14th February 1846 that she " says she is Strauss-sick—it makes her ill dissecting the beautiful story of the Crucifixion, and only the sight of the Christ image and picture make her endure it." A few years later, when her agnosticism had acquired the character of a more settled conviction, she wrote to Mme. Bodichon: " But I have faith in the working out of higher possibilities than the Catholic or any other Church has presented; and those who have strength to wait and endure are bound to accept no formula which their whole souls—their intelligence as well as their emotions—do not embrace with entire reverence. The ' highest calling and election ' is to do without opium, and live through all our pain with conscious clear-eyed courage." That was on 26th December 1860, just at the time of the second of the three controversies with which this book deals. Her words represent an attitude very widespread among thoughtful people of religious sensibility. And it was an attitude which any thoughtful Anglican might well have found as ominous as the loss of Newman in 1845. Just as Newman had come to believe that the true fulfilment of the Anglican principles to which he had given his life lay outside the Church of England, so did George Eliot believe that the true fulfilment of the highest Christian intuitions lay outside Christianity altogether. Both were great writers and master-minds; each was of an unimpeachable seriousness and moral intensity. Where they led in their opposite but equally unanglican directions there would be no lack of earnest spirits to follow.

Indeed the secularist pamphlets of the mid-Victorian period dispel any doubt one might entertain about the wide and growing appeal of George Eliot's approach to religion. One, for instance, entitled *Secularism and its Misrepresentatives* claimed that the majority of secularists " feel the mystery of the universe to be too profound for their minds to fathom, and humbly bow their head before it in conscious impotence and wonder; an attitude which displays far greater reverence than is manifested by the presumptuous dogmatism of the theologians." The key-word there is *reverence*. It meant that secularism could beat religion at its own game of worship.

Parallel with this current of thought, which suggested that the Christian religion was not sufficiently religious, went an even more damaging and more generally attractive one which suggested that Christianity was not sufficiently moral. An extreme exponent of this view was W. K. Clifford, the great mathematician, who died in 1879 at the age of thirty-four, having already won enduring fame. He proclaimed in his *Ethics of Religion* that " if men were no better than their religion, the world would be hell indeed." Of some of the sayings of Christ he remarked that " For a man who clearly felt and recognised the duty of intellectual honesty . . . it would be impossible to ascribe the profoundly immoral teachings of these texts to a true prophet or a worthy leader of humanity." Commenting on the Christian doctrine of the forgivenness of sins, he wrote " Can the favour of the Czar make guiltless the murderer of old men and women in Circassian valleys? Can the pardon of the

Sultan make clean the bloody hands of a Pasha? As little can God forgive sins against any man." Clifford was an extremist[1] and perhaps not many people agreed *in toto* with this line of reasoning. But comparable arguments in a slightly modified form are to be found over and over again. One of the most weighty and dignified of these was Mill's famous declaration about the immorality of the doctrine of eternal punishment.

Clifford and many others, of course, rejected religion in all its forms; and were probably, on that account, not among the Victorian writers most dangerous to the faith of believers. But other more cautious agnostics drew many away from belief in the creeds and from attendance at Church by means of a most attractive compromise, often known as " true Christianity". Lecky, for instance, the historian of European rationalism, wrote in the course of a chapter on ecclesiastical miracles the following very revealing passage:

" The spirit of the Fathers has incontestably faded. The days of Athanasius and Augustine have passed away never to return. The whole course of thought is flowing in another direction. The controversies of bygone centuries ring with a strange hollowness on the ear. But if turning from ecclesiastical historians, we apply the exclusively moral tests which the New Testament so invariably and so emphatically enforces, if. . . ."

Such a passage as this (which could easily be paralleled from other Agnostic writers) contained an insidious three-pronged attack against the faith of Anglicans. It insinuated

[1]Something of Clifford's own moral outlook can be gathered from the following characteristic letter written while he was staying in Spain: " As for this country, I think it requires to be colonised by the white man: the savages would gradually die out in his presence. The mark of a degraded race is clearly on their faces."

that as all good Englishmen agreed that it was the moral teaching of Christianity which really mattered, and as leading Victorian agnostics were almost invariably men of extreme respectability, faith and doctrine had become in the nineteenth century both incredible and otiose. Then it appropriated for the agnostic a type of argument which Anglicans and Protestants had been using for centuries and had thought of as their very own—the confident appeal away from ecclesiastical authority and tradition to the living words of the Gospels. Englishmen were so accustomed to this type of argument that it cost many of them a great effort to believe that it could ever produce a false conclusion. Not everyone by any means could see that such passages really assumed what they wished to prove. Finally, and perhaps most effective of all, was the implied connection between agnosticism and progress. Anglicanism and Protestantism were seen as only a temporary phase in the inevitable upward march of human reason from the barbarous superstitions of the Dark Ages to the pure rationalist position of Lecky and his friends. Nothing is drearier than to be merely an unstable adolescent stage in the growing-pains of emergent humanity. Men like Lecky and T. H. Huxley made many an anxious Christian wonder whether after all his belief represented no more than that.

The much-discussed Victorian belief in progress is often misunderstood because it is assumed that it was always an optimistic belief. It would perhaps be nearer the mark to say that many Victorians believed in the inevitability of continuing process. It was difficult for them to grasp imaginatively the idea a trend could ever be reversed. Agnostics looked out with exultation, Christians looked out with alarm upon a world in which dogmatic belief seemed to be becoming constantly less. The decline of religion in the future seemed as inevitable to Tennyson as it did to Huxley, but the imaginary certainty was as painful to the one as it was pleasant to the other.

This sense of irreversible process which was so comforting to the agnostics had also a great influence upon controversies within the Church. It gave confidence to the innovators and all those who put a minimal interpretation on the Church's doctrines. It meant that men like Jowett and Colenso, even though apparently belonging to a harried minority, looked forward serenely to a future when the mere passage of time would place them in the majority. While those who like Phillpotts and Pusey were trying to maintain a rigidly dogmatic system, however strong their faith might be, felt themselves to be solitary Canutes resisting well-nigh irresistible tides of opinion. This is one reason among others why the controversies can be so misleading. It was sometimes the poor persecuted eccentrics who felt hopeful; it was sometimes the official and prosecuting party who felt beset by dangers. Rebels within the Church who wished to modify or discard the Church's doctrines shared with Agnostics a bracing conviction that all history had been preparing for the bold innovations they were now making. An extreme but by no means untypical case is quoted by that notable recorder of Victorian eccentricity C. M. Davies from a lecture delivered to a tiny agnostic sect, the South London Secularists: " The Roman Catholics begat the Protestants, the Protestants begat the Denominationalists, the Denominationalists begat the Deists, the Deists begat the Infidels, and Infidels begat sensible men [i.e. the South London Secularists]." *Parturiunt montes. . . .*

A notable book which combines a great many scattered Victorian tendencies in a single volume is *Robert Elsmere*. Here we have the " inevitable " triumph of a new and simpler type of religion. Gladstone, who reviewed the book

at length in the *Nineteenth Century*, was deeply intrigued
by the absence of reasoned argument against traditional
Christianity and in favour of the new faith. Of the hero's
feeble attempt to defend Christianity against agnostic attack,
he said, not unfairly, that it was " a fictitious battle, on the
one side a paean, on the other a blank", and he added, " a
great creed with the testimony of eighteen centuries at its
back cannot find an articulate word." *Robert Elsmere* is a
long and conscientious book, and the truth of Gladstone's
point is a measure of the sublime confidence of its author.
It was *obvious* to her that traditional Christianity could not
long survive; it was *obvious* that some system such as Robert
Elsmere's own must soon take its place. There is nothing
original in his new doctrine. It is merely Christianity
with certain ideas, such as the Incarnation, sacraments and
miracles, left out. These things, of course, were deliberately
abandoned as having had their day. (Half-way through the
book the hero bangs the table and says " Miracles do not
happen "—it is like a Calvinist conversion, a sudden self-
verifying message from above, something beyond the reach
of argument.) But one theological idea was dropped over-
board and hardly noticed. That was original sin. *Robert
Elsmere* tacitly assumes, and in this it is a fair guide to much
progressive thought of the time, that ignorance, not sin, is
the cause of evil in human beings.

It was this underlying conviction, more than anything
else, that enabled both agnostics, and those, like Mrs.
Humphrey Ward who clung on to a few shreds of faith while
accepting most of the current agnostic assumptions, to take
such a cheerful view of future prospects. For anyone who
maintains that in the future human society will become
prosperous, just and happy, has to face the question, " Why,
if men are capable of all this, has it not been so in the past? "
To this question men like Leslie Stephen or Mill or G. H.

Lewes had a confident answer ready. Education is spreading, and knowledge is increasing as never before. Their whole intellectual position, their political hopes and their religious denials were based upon the idea of a great mass of certain, verifiable knowledge, which had grown rapidly and would go on growing. And this, of course, would lead to a constant improvement in the moral goodness as well as in the prosperity of the whole people.

It is here, perhaps, that the indispensable word agnostic is liable to mislead us. The word itself suggests doubt, uncertainty, scepticism. These were qualities conspicuously lacking in the men we now habitually think of as the leading Victorian agnostics—T. H. Huxley, Herbert Spencer, Leslie Stephen and Charles Darwin. Men like these believed that in each separate field of inquiry, in physics, in anthropology, in political economy, the wonderful new techniques of detailed observation and controlled generalisation were producing certain results. They rejected religion, not so much because they doubted, as because the huge and ever-increasing mass of certain knowledge made a supposed divine revelation almost redundant.

The real doubters were very different. They were men like Clough, who ineffectively hankered after a religious belief they could not quite accept; or men like Tennyson, who clung on to their religious faith with the utmost difficulty. In either case, they were as a rule men of profoundly conservative instincts, for whom the relentless changes of the nineteenth century were a nightmare. It was no "agnostic", but Tennyson, the devout Poet Laureate, who wrote,

Behold, we know not anything.

It was Tennyson who described himself, as Huxley, Spencer and the rest would never have dreamt of doing, as:

Doctrine and Authority: The Agnostic Version

An infant crying in the night:
An infant crying for the light:
And with no language but a cry.

Leslie Stephen expressed the sentiments of many agnostics when he said that doubt stopped short at the findings of Euclid, or Archimedes, or Newton. He did not mean that we ought not to doubt these things, as a theologian might say that we ought not to doubt the Athanasian creed. He meant that, for a man of enough intelligence to understand how their conclusions were reached, it was impossible to doubt them. They were like the multiplication table, self-evident. Doubt, as conceived by Stephen and by many others, might be compared to the sea. It might range over most of the intellectual world, just as the sea covers most of the earth; for men were weak and their knowledge small, when compared to the totality of possible knowledge. But just as we are not disturbed because the sea is more extensive than the land, and do not worry for a moment about a universal flood, so did Stephen range freely over continents of knowledge, rejoicing in their inviolable safety from attack. He could not imagine a time when even Newton and Euclid would be questioned, when what he would have considered the most obvious moral platitude would start a controversy. In one sense, the mid-Victorian agnostics lived before the flood.

It will easily be seen that such an attitude was bound to have repercussions in the sphere of religious dogma. For religious dogma was unmistakably dogma, that is to say, however convincing the reasons presented for believing it might be, yet it was not susceptible of proof, in the sense in which scientists and mathematicians understood the word, and it was evidently *possible* to disbelieve it. In previous times thoughtful men had realised that almost all our ideas and opinions have to be taken on trust, in some degree; so it had not seemed unreasonable to take religious doctrines on trust also, if they could show themselves to be trustworthy. But the sceptical spirit of Montaigne and Pascal was utterly alien to the confident minds of Stephen and Huxley, however reverently they might sometimes quote them. Vast tracts of knowledge were certain; therefore why bother with religious doctrines which were, at the best, speculative?

Christians found this challenge peculiarly hard to meet, because so many of them really agreed, openly or secretly, that the great and increasing body of knowledge, of which the agnostics boasted, was incontrovertible. Tennyson was no consistent thinker, and the quotation that follows is hardly consistent with the previous one. But his inconsistency is bound up with his great value as a witness. For he expressed so perfectly the varying moods and intellectual fashions of his numerous contemporaries, who both clung to religion and experienced doubt and worry. The widespread nervousness of Christians before the advance of secular knowledge can be gathered from these extraordinary lines:

> *I think we are not wholly brain,*
> *Magnetic mockeries . . . .*
> *Not only cunning casts in clay:*
> *Let science prove we are, and then*
> *What matters science unto men,*
> *At least to me?*

Two words immediately strike the reader here, the word "science" and the word "prove." We would expect (if we may ignore the verse form for a moment) something on the lines of "Let scientists say we are." But for Tennyson as for so many bewildered Christians, science had become a terrifying and unassailable oracle, of which actual fallible human scientists were only the servants. You could not question what science said; you could not argue about it; you could not enquire whether the matter was really one that science was competent to decide. You could only, if the verdict was too bitter to be borne, turn your back on it and try to forget it, as Tennyson proposed to do here.

The consequence was that agnostics were able to be dogmatic without knowing it, for they believed that their science, their anthropology, their political economy and the rest were simply making statements of the order " Two and two are four." Christians, clinging with various degrees of uneasiness to the traditional doctrines, generally saw no reason to question this implicit claim. Both sides on the whole accepted the truth of the contrast, on the one hand religious dogma based wholly on faith, on the other an agnostic system based wholly on reason. In the circumstances the temptation felt by worried, thoughtful Christians to jettison any article of their faith which came under attack as being barbarous or useless or outmoded was very strong indeed. It is essential to remember this, in assessing the policies of men like Phillpotts and Pusey who strove to resist this minimising tendency. They felt that time was running short, that external enemies of religion were growing so powerful that doubters and possible enemies within the fold could not be tolerated. They might seem outwardly to be acting with irresistible authority against the weak. But they knew that it was not so. They were acting with reckless courage against overwhelming odds; and their fierce attitude to those they considered traitors might be compared to the action of the Home Office in arresting aliens in May 1940.

So it was that, throughout the period with which this book deals, the uneasiness of Anglicans and the self-confidence of agnostics reacted upon each other, so that each was intensified. Anglican uneasiness could take several different forms. It could be exasperated and ferocious, as with Phillpotts; it could be gloomy and fatalistic, as with Tennyson; it could be almost buried under a flood of deeply-felt rhetoric, as with Gladstone. But the agnostics never ceased to be aware of its presence, and some of them became very skilful in penetrating its disguises; it was inevitable that their awareness of it should strengthen their conviction that the future, both intellectual and practical, belonged to them alone.

In particular, they were able to turn two current Protestant *idées reçues* with deadly effect against the Christians. Like most *idées reçues*, these were as vague and hard to formulate as they were pervasive and influential. But the first ran something like this: Protestantism is the religion of progress; we have climbed up out of the childish superstitions of the Dark Ages into a higher, more adult religious phase. This gave an easy opening to agnostics to say that they represented a yet higher stage than Protestantism in the upward march of the religious and moral consciousness of humanity. Thus Lecky could write of the Reformation: " There certainly never has been a movement which, in its ultimate results, has contributed so largely to the emancipation of the human mind from all superstitious terrors as the Reformation. It formed a multitude of churches, in which the spirit of qualified and partial scepticism that had long been a source of anarchy, might expatiate with freedom, and be allied with the spirit of order. It rejected an immense proportion of the dogmatic and ritualistic conceptions that had almost covered the whole field of religion, and rendered possible that steady movement by which theology has since then been gravitating towards the moral faculty. It above all diminished the prominence of the clergy; and thus prepared the way for that general secularisation of the

European intellect, which is such a marked characteristic of modern civilisation." Praise of their beloved Reformation based on the assumption that all religion was, of course, rubbish, was naturally wormwood to Protestants. And the passage also well illustrates that easy, confident, superior tone shared by so many leading agnostics, which Christians found so frightening.

The second *idée reçue* was that religion was a social necessity to maintain the moral standards of society, and to check anarchy and crime. This doctrine laid Christians open to a series of devastating questions. What about the very " religious " Dark Ages, which were, on your own showing, times of desperate crime, stagnation and superstition? How do you square your continual talk of moral progress and improvement with the undoubted fact that the number of people in England with no religion at all (in your narrow and incomplete understanding of the word) is greater than ever before? And how, if religion is indeed the sole guardian of morality, does it come about that we, the leading agnostic citizens, follow so much more conscientiously than most Christians the moral precepts of the Gospels? You believe in progress? Well then, do you not see that you represent the past and we represent the future?

Many Christians had made themselves exceedingly vulnerable to such arguments. If the Protestants were somewhat more vulnerable to them than High Churchmen, High Churchmen had enough special extra worries of their own to make the balance roughly even. They had, for instance, more to fear from state interference and legal decisions. Indeed, all who tried to maintain or enforce any kind of Anglican orthodoxy in the mid-Victorian period took on a formidable task, beset with impressive agnostic intellectual achievements, hampered by the uncomprehending action of the State and its judges, secretly frightened **by** their suspicion that a trend away from their own type of faith could never be reversed. As we come to consider these terrible domestic disputes between Anglicans we should always remember the power of the fears they all shared. Chief among these was the vision of the agnostic party as a compact, successful, efficient, implacable *tertius gaudens*.

CHAPTER THREE

The Erastian Crisis

THE SIMPLE outline of what was to prove a very complicated affair—the Gorham case of 1850, was as follows. Gorham, an elderly clergyman, suspected by his bishop, Phillpotts of Exeter, of not holding the correct Anglican doctrine of baptismal regeneration, was indicted for heresy, found guilty before the ecclesiastical courts (Court of Arches) and acquitted on appeal by the Privy Council with the concurrence of its assessors the Archbishops of Canterbury and York. Though, as we shall see, other issues in the case ultimately became more fundamental to the life of the Church of England, the dispute originally concerned baptismal regeneration; and it will perhaps be appropriate to summarise the various views of it.

The formularies of the Church of England state that baptism washes away original sin, the hereditary taint common to the whole human race, and regenerates the soul, that is, makes it a recipient of divine grace. Now according to Phillpotts and the High Church party this must mean in the case of an infant, who can have committed no personal sin, that once baptised he is certainly in a state of grace, as original sin, the only obstacle to grace in this case, has been washed away. Baptism is a divinely instituted method of applying the merits of redemption, the power of Christ's blood, to the individual soul. And so, the argument ran, to cast doubt upon this is to cast doubt upon the power and the mercy of God; moreover, to cast doubt upon it would open the door to worry, uncertainty, and despair, for if baptism were not always and absolutely effective, no one could be sure of its efficacy in his own case or in that of his children.

The opposition to this view is not so easy to analyse. Gorham himself was a Calvinist, but there were a multitude of Low Churchmen and even liberals who sided with Gorham against Phillpotts without being Calvinist. Gorham believed that God, by His own unsearchable will, and for no reason explicable in human categories, had chosen out certain souls for salvation and rejected others. Baptism was the proper, divinely instituted sign of this election, but the baptism of an infant was not an infallible guide to the unknowable fact of election in any given case. To suggest that it was, was to set a mere human act and intention above the irreversible decrees of God. The language of the baptismal service, which spoke of the regeneration of the child's soul, must be interpreted, like the language of the Burial Service, as a statement of devout hope, not of certain fact. When the clergyman spoke the words of the Burial Service, he was not proclaiming that he knew for certain that the dead man's soul was saved, for that would be to usurp God's sole right to judge; he was expressing a pious hope, and so he ought to be when he baptised a child.

Each doctrine in fact in its different way aimed to safeguard the supremacy of the divine judgment over human opinion. To Phillpotts the effects of baptism were certain, not because baptism was an official act of the Church, but because it was a divine ordinance with a divine promise attached to it. Gorham agreed that baptism was a divine ordinance, but held that its effects were conditional, dependent upon a yet greater divine ordinance, the unknowable election or reprobation of the individual soul.

These two views, and various modifications of them, like contrasting views on so many other theological points, had existed side by side in the Church of England for centuries, and no controversy between them had ever been mortal. It was not to be mortal now. The importance of the crisis of 1850 did not lie in the realm of sacramental theology. The great question posed by the Gorham case was " Is the Church of England primarily a church, that is, an autonomous spiritual body dispensing doctrine and law, or is it a body dependent on the State, and destined always to alter its message in accordance with the changing pressures of national policy or popular opinion? " When the Privy Council reversed the decision of the ecclesiastical courts and declared Gorham justified, it was not really deciding on the merits of a controversy about baptism, which, perhaps, few of its members fully understood. It was maintaining the idea of the Church as a national institution against the idea of the Church as an autonomous body. To this end it had no need to decide in favour of any given theory of baptismal regeneration. It merely needed to veto any attempt by a bishop to impose a view of it, however traditional, however rational, however clearly contained in the Church's formularies, upon any recalcitrant clergyman. It was deciding in favour of national comprehensiveness; it would no doubt have decided in favour of Phillpotts if (as might easily have been the case) Gorham had been a bishop attempting to impose a Calvinist doctrine. Thus Phillpotts and Gorham were each equally opposed to the spirit of dogmatic indifference which prompted the Privy Council and which was so widespread throughout the nation. It was the accident of their positions, not their doctrines, which produced a decision in favour of the one and against the other.

Comprehensiveness as against dogmatism is generally a popular cause in England. But the Privy Council's decision implied a great deal more; that the Church must be what the government or the people wished it to be; therefore (on this view) it could not be the guardian of a divine message to be preached in season and out of season. The State could change it; the State, it was implied, had created it; the State could bring it to an end.

Now of course such a claim was a commonplace in the long vista of fifteen hundred years since Christianity emerged from the catacombs, and found in Constantine the most generous and embarrassing of allies. But the present instance of an age-old claim—the claim of the State to rule the Church—had this exceptional feature. When the Privy Council promulgated its decision the Archbishops of Canterbury and York were assessors to the Court, and concurred in its decision. The supporters of Phillpotts felt that it was one thing to be dominated by the State and another to welcome the domination. They were conceding, in theory perhaps, only a right of the civil courts to interpret the formularies of the Church, but in fact, as it seemed to some, the right to alter and control them. For if baptismal regeneration was not taught in the Church's formularies, of what doctrine could it be said that it certainly was taught there? To Phillpotts and his supporters, as we shall see, the craven surrender, or the sincere concurrence (whichever it was) of the archbishops, while the traditional and indispensable faith of the Church was being repudiated, was far more serious than any claim made by the State, any decision of secular courts, could ever be. For them it meant that the rot was working from within; the fortress which had endured for eighteen centuries was being betrayed by its own commanders. The leaders of the Church seemed to be saying to the persecuting State what Ugolino's children said to their father as they begged him to relieve his hunger by feeding upon them: "You bestowed this wretched garment of flesh upon us, and it is for you to consume it."

It was with some such sense of approaching a desperate crisis that in the early months of 1850 a series of small, private meetings were attended by some of the ablest and most influential Churchmen of the day. Among them were Gladstone, Manning, R. I. Wilberforce, brother of Samuel Wilberforce, Bishop of Oxford, Pusey, Keble and James Hope, later known as Hope-Scott.

At first they all imagined that they thought alike; they certainly all believed that the English Church, to which they were bound by strong ties of upbringing and personal loyalty, must maintain the creeds if it was to deserve their loyalty. Yet the crisis was to reveal a crucial difference in their underlying attitudes. Manning, Hope and Robert Wilberforce were soon to go over to Rome. The rest remained Anglicans all their lives.

If we discount minor differences, there were four divergent views of the problem represented at these meetings. The first, that of those who were soon to become Roman Catholics, was summarised in Hope's remark, " I suppose we are all agreed that if the Church of England does not undo this, we must join the Church of Rome." To him, as to Manning, the Privy Council decision provided a perfectly clear test of the claims of the Church of England to be regarded as a Catholic Church. It seemed to them obvious that a Church could not be regarded as Catholic unless it would itself claim the title. That title had been implicitly denied by the Privy Council decision. If the Church did not repudiate that decision and affirm its claim to the title of Catholic, the whole case would go by default, and those who had desired to be both Catholic and Anglican would have no choice but to take refuge in the Church which unquestionably did teach the doctrines enshrined in the creeds.

Keble's view was utterly different. Manning later reported Keble as having said, " if the Church of England were to fail, it would be found in my parish." Whether or not the words are an exact record of what Keble said, they really do convey in epigrammatic form the essence of his doctrine. Keble differed from his chief colleagues in the Oxford Movement in one important respect. While Newman, Hurrell Froude and later Pusey believed that they were resuscitating a tradition of Catholicism in the Church of England which had been dormant since the seventeenth century, Keble believed that he was carrying on a tradition which had never been forgotten. He once said of the Oxford Movement doctrines that they were what he had always been taught, that is, in his childhood before 1810, over twenty years before the Oxford Movement began. Keble's was a profoundly conservative spirit. He had been brought up in a tradition, his deeply religious spirit had made that tradition his own. He had done battle for it in the early years of the Oxford Movement. In 1850 he was in his fifty-eighth year, and he intended to die in the same tradition. If others abandoned it, if the bishops would not speak for it, he was sad, but his firmness remained unshaken. For Manning and Hope as for Newman, the Church of England deserved loyalty only so long as it could show how it fitted into the scheme of a universal Church. For Keble faith in the Church of England was primary, and the idea of a universal Church was something that had to be fitted into the Anglican system. For Keble the whole affair provided much grief but no uncertainty, and no intellectual difficulty at all.

Pusey's case was quite different again. Unlike Keble, he had adopted High Church doctrines, by conscious adult choice after very careful thought and study. He was learned, had indeed become Professor of Hebrew at Oxford before he was thirty. He had satisfied himself that the Church of England was, historically speaking, Catholic and a true portion of the universal Church. It was therefore literally impossible for it to deny the faith. It was indeed a matter of great concern to him if the Queen, the Prime Minister, the clergy, the laity or the bishops denied the faith, but not one of them, nor all of them together, could commit the Church to heresy. He could no more accept a denial by the Church of its acceptance of the true faith than one can believe a man who says, " I am not here." For him the Church of England was not primary. The universal Church was primary; and that was now divided into fragments. Therefore no one, neither the Pope nor the Archbishop of Canterbury nor anyone else could formulate doctrine with final authority. The final authority lay in the pronouncements of the undivided Church of the first Christian centuries. Obviously these could not now be changed. Neither could anything happen to change the Catholic status of a Church which, like the Church of England, already possessed it.

All these three views were consistent, rational and intelligible. The fourth, that of Gladstone, was uncertain and obscure. It must have seemed at first that his thoughts were similar to those of Manning and Hope. When told of the Privy Council judgment, Gladstone, according to Manning, who visited him when he was ill in bed, " starting up and throwing out his arms, exclaimed, ' The Church of England is gone unless it releases itself by some authoritative act'." But when the whole group met together to agree upon and sign a document of protest against the Privy Council's decision, and the Archbishops' concurrence in it, Gladstone refused to sign, and according to one account he explained his refusal by asking, " Do you think that I, a Privy Councillor, could sign? " And this refusal is the more surprising when one reflects that the document was an extremely moderate one: for it stated that "All measures *consistent with the present legal position of the Church* ought to be taken without delay to obtain an authoritative declaration by the Church of the doctrine of Holy Baptism impugned by the recent sentence." The phrase italicised must have seemed to some Anglo-Catholics distinctly timorous. For it was precisely the legal position which they objected to—the fact that the State had given itself the legal right to decide the Church's doctrine for it and to override the Church's own leaders. If the essential issue was Erastian control of the Church, just as much as it was baptismal regeneration, such a document might have been thought to abandon half the case from the start. However, Gladstone would not sign, and it must be admitted that a politician is not in a favourable position to resist Erastian tendencies in the State. Gladstone never attempted a detailed defence of the consistency of his conduct on this occasion. In a letter of 14th June, 1850, he described the Privy Council as "contrary to the very first principles of the gospel." Thereafter he relapsed into public silence on the question.

Differences such as these, among opponents of the Privy Council judgment, though important were by no means obvious. There were much more apparent differences between those who welcomed it. Gorham and his Calvinist supporters naturally regarded the judgment as a victory for them. But Calvinism was far from being a dominant force in the Church of England, and they could not help realising that the grounds upon which this favourable decision had been reached were quite alien to Calvinist principles. The decision was based not on Calvinist dogma but on the evasion of all dogma. It did not aim to impose a formula but to impose an open question.

The real gainers from the Privy Council decision were the Broad Church party. For them, just as much as for the despondent High Churchmen and the defiant Phillpotts, the decision and the archbishops' concurrence in it represented a landmark. They saw it as a deliverance from a great danger, and an earnest of future benefits for the Church of England. Observers of this school said, in effect, " Christendom is full of churches, and each has its own private dogmas, often differing from the dogmas of all other churches; these dogmas then are forces working for divisions and hatred. How foolish for us Anglicans to set up our own collection of dogmas in opposition to all the others. You talk about the historic faith of Christendom, but are we not Protestants and did we not deliberately break away from that in the 16th century? The Roman Church is usually considered the guardian of traditional orthodoxy, and we have never heard that the Church of England now or in the past or in any imaginable future agrees very well with the Church of Rome. Very well then; instead of playing all these people at their own game, we have our own peculiar glory, and that is that we are not dogmatic, do not insist on inessentials, and being aware of the fallibility of mortals, we must not allow the exponents of any one theological idea, however apparently sound, to cast doubt on the loyalty of any other party. You say we are opening the door to Calvinists, Ultramontanes, and men who are not Christians at all. Well, if Calvinists and Ultramontanes are willing to join, or to remain within, the Church of England, then by all means let them. They may acquire a little of our tolerance. Let us exclude nobody who does not exclude himself."

Each side of the argument was in its own way rational and compelling. It all depended on first principles. But Dean Stanley, perhaps the leading exponent of this view, was essentially a practical man. And he realised that the Church needed something more to hold it together than a general agreement among its members never to push things to extremes. The Church, however tolerant and comprehensive, aspires to be not a mere collection of bricks, but a structure. Where was the cement to be found? Phillpotts and the High Church party, Gorham and the Calvinists, each in their opposing ways found it in doctrinal agreement. The Broad Church school of Dean Stanley found it partly in the Englishness of the English Church, in its liturgy, its parish ethos, and the subtle tradition of religious sensibility inspired by Prayer Book and Authorised Version. But recognising that all these were still not quite sufficient, in default of doctrinal agreement, they found the final bond of Church unity in the State. But here they were glad to see that there was no occasion to take sides. The highest legal authority of the State, sitting side by side with the archbishops, had arrived at a unanimous verdict in favour of comprehensiveness. It seemed like an overwhelming and permanent victory.

In an institution like the English Church, few victories are permanent, for no decision of whatever authority, ecclesiastical or secular, is held by those who oppose it to be binding. The defeat of dogma in 1850 initiated a gradual reaction which culminated some 15 years later in the Colenso case, when the bishops at last successfully defied the State. No responsible leader, even of the High Church party, ever hoped for complete independence of the State; perhaps few in their hearts desired it. But all those who cared for the Church's doctrinal foundations, all those who were unwilling to see the Crown or the Privy Council as an ultimate religious authority, took warning by the Gorham case. Their efforts finally bore fruit in the establishment of uneasy equilibrium, which has proved unexpectedly stable for nearly a hundred years—an equilibrium admirably exemplified by the Prayer Book controversy of 1928. It is this: the State decides, and then leaders of the Church occasionally, if they feel really strongly, do not question the right of the State to decide but simply refuse to obey. The State ignores this disobedience. The absolute power of the State, as revealed in the decision of 1850, was over-thrown without a revolution, without a change of written principles, because it had come to seem to many people crushing and arbitrary. But all this was in the future.

II

The Church of England is the home of an infinite number of shades of opinion. And so it is inevitable that when a full scale controversy occurs, and everyone who cares for such things is driven to support one side or the other, there should be a great difference of opinion among allies. In this case the contrast between the protagonists and their followers was particularly marked. Bishop Phillpotts was 55 years of age in 1833, the year in which it is generally reckoned that the Oxford Movement began. He was a man of keen intellect, strong will, considerable self-confidence. He was not an original thinker nor much given to introspection. He used his high mental powers as a barrister does. He produced a powerfully logical argument based on the precise letter of the law, and then backed it by a strong emotional appeal. His writings lack that wide sweep and ranging intellectual curiosity which distinguished the works of Newman, and in lesser degree of his colleagues in the Oxford Movement. Phillpotts never threw in his lot with the Oxford Movement; both his traditions and his experience made it very difficult for him to understand it. The Oxford party in its early years was a young man's party, and Phillpotts was one of the last men in England likely to undergo a change of mind and heart after middle age. The old eighteenth century High Church party, of which Phillpotts was the last distinguished representative, fought side by side with the Puseyites because their enemies were on the whole the same. They did not often take their eyes off the enemy to glance sideways and consider the principles of the men beside them, and when they did they were puzzled. Phillpotts and those for whom he spoke had never felt the lure of Rome, nor did they worry about Biblical criticism and the spread of infidel ideas from Germany. They assumed that old England was what it always had been, and High Churchmen though they were, they still owed much to the profoundly nationalistic Protestantism which after three centuries of massive strength was now at last beginning to show signs of weakness. But the signs were apparent only to the very discriminating, to those with the rare gift of anticipating future currents of public opinion. It was a gift which Phillpotts did not possess. Both the churchmanship and the political outlook of Phillpotts had come to have a very old-fashioned air by the 1840's. He had been brought up in a privileged class of a privileged Church. His income from Church sources was enormous, and he was able to ensure that his numerous children shared in the material benefits of his ecclesiastical position. He had been the target of popular resentment, expressed in the most practical form of stones and broken windows at the time of the Reform Bill of 1832. He stood, as so many of his eighteenth century predecessors had done, for " Church and King;" a formula which so often really means " King—and Church." He had, admittedly, an obstinate and self-important temperament, but his obstinacy was all on the side of the powers that be. During the first seventy years or so of his life no one can have imagined that he would ever be a rebel.

But despite his worldly streak, he was a man of principle.

And in the circumstances of the mid-nineteenth century, a man of principle was very liable to come into collision with the State upon religious questions. There could be no more striking demonstration of this than the case of Phillpotts, privileged, traditionalist, insular, patriotic, deeply loyal to throne and to establishment, a man devoted to the *status quo*, from which all his life he had derived such authority and profit. Such men are not rebels for nothing.

No degree of privilege or of social conformity caused Phillpotts to forget his most fundamental conviction, that the essentials of the Christian faith were unalterable. He was eventually driven by this conviction to defy the throne and the courts and to excommunicate the Archbishop of Canterbury for concurring in the State's heretical judgment. On 7th August 1850, when, it seemed, he had finally lost his battle, he wrote " His Grace's [Canterbury's] complicity in this awful work is thus consummated by the Privy Council's decision and I cannot hold communion with him. I cannot communicate *in sacris* with him." This seemed at the time to everyone, even to Phillpotts himself, only a magnificent gesture in defeat. But Phillpotts was to live into extreme old age, and to see, when he could no longer take an active part in public affairs, a partial reversal of defeat, when the bishops in a body defied the Crown in the Colenso case. Though approaching his ninetieth year he was able to sign what amounted to a manifesto of defiance, and to reflect perhaps that to stand out for a forlorn hope on principle sometimes brings unexpected rewards.

The other protagonist, Gorham, was in some ways curiously like his opponent. He too was a man of great courage, prone to anger, and mentally very efficient without being original. The great crisis of his life found him no longer young: he was sixty-three in 1850. It is a good illustration of the haphazard nature of Anglican authority

51

and the elements of chance which govern its great controversies that Gorham should have been preaching an identical doctrine for nearly forty years unchallenged; and should then have suddenly become the central figure in a celebrated controversy. Yet in one sense fate had not chosen its victim ill. Unlike the authors of *Essays and Reviews* and unlike Colenso whose doctrines were to be the subject of the controversies which followed, Gorham knew exactly what he believed, understood all the most subtle implications of his belief, and was by temperament a lover of controversy. Both Phillpotts and Gorham suffered much through the Gorham case. But nevertheless, one has the feeling that when they were disputing together, orally and in print, they were having the time of their lives. And the purely intellectual pleasure of the contest was heightened for each,— for Phillpotts by the conviction that he was acting in this latter age of infidelity and indifference with the stern, yet loving care for his flock which a bishop of the fourth century might have shown; and for Gorham by the sense of suffering insult and calumny for his faith. Both were men of fierce conviction. But while Phillpotts was maintaining a system which he conceived to be traditional and unchanging, Gorham was the kind of man who inclines to believe that, if he himself were to fail, truth might perish utterly from the earth. He saw himself as the pioneer of a new freedom. " I have been called by Providence," he wrote in his published account of his lengthy debate with the bishop, " not merely to maintain my personal right, but virtually to struggle for purity of doctrine, and for liberty of conscience, on behalf of a very large body of the clergy."

It is natural that the weak should look round for protectors in time of trouble; it is natural that an accused man should seize any advantages that the law may allow him. But in appealing for the State to defend him, Gorham was soon insensibly driven to a much more Erastian position than was really in accord with his own principles. As a strict Calvinist, he was no more friendly to a comprehensive, indifferentist view of the Church of England than Phillpotts was. Erastianism, or the belief that Church government is vested by divine right in the State, does not agree very well with Calvinism. Or rather, the two might conceivably agree if Calvin's ideal theocratic state were realised, but obviously nothing could be further from such an ideal than the actual state of affairs in Victorian England. The unnoticed but relentless pressure of external events drove Gorham who theoretically believed only in the inner light, to the advocacy of a rigid control of doctrine by the State. As we have already seen in the case of Gladstone on the opposite side, throughout this case, and indeed thoughout the period with which this book deals, the spirit of Erastianism seems almost to acquire a personal identity, and to insert itself into the most unlikely mental crannies, against the declared and patently sincere intention of men. That is one reason why the deliberate and consistent Erastians, like Dean Stanley, had such an advantage over all other parties.

III

The argument that was spread throughout the Church and the country began with two men face to face in a single room. Gorham had advertised in the press for a curate " free from Tractarian error," and the bishop, seeing the advertisement, though by no means wholly a Tractarian himself, considered the phrase ominous and perhaps suggestive of heretical doctrines. When a little later Gorham was presented by the Lord Chancellor to a living near Exeter, Phillpotts refused to institute without a previous doctrinal examination. The first of a series of examinations took place in December 1847. On several days the examinations lasted for some eight hours, and on one occasion for something like twelve hours. They faced each other, and hour after hour, both orally and in writing, they lacerated each other's arguments. Sometimes sittings did not end until one or other of the disputants was nearing physical collapse. Yet, so far as we know, neither of them ever once mentioned the issue that was to be for the public, both learned and ignorant, the crucial question of the case—the Royal supremacy, its powers and its limits. The demonstration of the power of the State in matters of doctrine was to provide the second great blow to the nascent Anglo-Catholic movement, comparable in its force to the blow it sustained in 1845 when Newman left it and bequeathed in *The Development of Christian Doctrine* the most subtle, comprehensive and persuasive, as well as one of the friendliest, of all the attacks ever launched upon the Anglo-Catholic position. It was this issue, springing suddenly to life directly through the Gorham case (without which it might have been allowed to slumber peacefully on for a further period) which produced a crisis in the life of Gladstone, which was the occasion of providing Rome with that rarest of dignitaries, a convert primate and cardinal, and it was this issue that was never mentioned by Gorham or by Phillpotts in all those weary hours and days.

How far, one wonders, was it in their minds? Neither of them can have guessed how celebrated the cause which they were inaugurating would become. As they faced each other, so opposite in their principles, so similar in their character and their gifts, each may have been aware of a personal crisis, hardly as yet of a crisis of that Church in which each in his way deeply believed. To Phillpotts, with his wider vision, and his consciousness of being a great public figure, far more famous than most bishops, glimpses of the future came earlier than to Gorham. He was always keenly aware of his authority as a bishop, but he had still to learn how narrow are the practical limits of a bishop's authority in England, once public interest has been aroused, and the power of the State invoked.

When the dispute between the two men in a room together was over, having reached no satisfactory conclusion, the affair had to pass first to the Court of Arches, an ecclesiastical court with a lay judge, and thence to the Privy Council. For both courts the case presented issues of extreme difficulty. Sir Herbert Jenner Fust, who gave judgment in the Court of Arches, felt little confidence in the soundness of his decision in favour of Phillpotts. And one judge, Sir James Parke, actually enquired whether the decision was a legal or a theological one. This puzzled query, which in the mouth of a learned judge certainly has its comic side, nevertheless went to the core of the matter and exposed the whole logical weakness of the system. For if it was a theological decision, how could it have authority, coming from an untrained layman, who derived his right to judge merely from a secular office? And if it was a legal decision, how could it be binding upon conscience? Moreover, if, as the judges after some hesitation assumed, it really was a legal decision only that they were asked to give, then it was a question of interpreting certain sixteenth century formularies. Lawyers and judges would naturally treat these as they would treat the betting laws; they would judge not by their general drift or by the (highly speculative) intentions of the men who framed them, but by their exact words. As Johnson observed "The rights of nations and of kings sink into questions of grammar, if grammarians discuss them." A similar nemesis, in the Gorham case and in later controversies, attended the decision of religious questions by lawyers.

Very often the men who were called upon to judge realised this to the full. And it was largely due to this realisation that their decisions were so slow, so lacking in decisive confidence and so contradictory. It soon became common form in Victorian ecclesiastical cases for decisions to be reversed on appeal. But in the 1840's people had no idea that this would prove to be so. And it is a little strange, when one considers all that was said during the dispute about the ecclestical power of the State, how one party considered it as the saviour of a Protestant nation from sacerdotal oppression, and the other regarded it as a grim semi-pagan tyrant, and an enemy to the true faith—it is a little strange to find how ineffective and halting the intervention of the State actually was. But it most certainly does not follow from this that the party of Phillpotts and the party of Gorham were unrealistic in being deeply concerned about the State's legal power to decide. Perhaps it did not, in the end, matter very much how the State decided. The life of the Church of England went on much the same after the decision as before. If it was the occasion of distinguished Anglicans leaving the Church of their birth for Rome, it can be argued that the logic of their position would sooner or later have led them to take this step in any case. Anglicanism went on much the same, just as the rejection of the revised Prayer Book by Parliament in 1928 did not prevent those who wished from using it. But what did and does matter is whether the State decides religious questions, and by what authority.

A few people said this clearly at the time. Thus Binney, in a very intelligent book on the Gorham case written from a Congregationalist point of view, scored a telling point against the evangelical Anglican *Christian Observer*. Why was it, he asked, that, before the judgment in the Court of Arches the *Christian Observer* expressed every confidence both in the competence of the tribunal and in the successful issue of the case, but after this judgment went against Gorham, attacked not only its substance but its validity. Where was the sense, in Binney's words, of " condemning one layman for judging a question of divinity, and appealing from him to a dozen others " [i.e., to the Privy Council]? Such objections were in logic very formidable indeed, and they could have been made, *mutatis mutandis*, to a very large proportion of all the articles and opinions that the case called forth. Incidentally they were the very same objections that Roman Catholics felt.

There was also published a most remarkable document, entitled *Letter to a Clergyman of the Evangelical School* by A. B. The author accepted the judgment of the Court of Arches that Gorham was heretical and had no right to be instituted in his living. Writing before the reversal of this judgment by the Privy Council he naturally assumed that the decision favourable to his own views would stand. His concern in the letter is for a clergyman who believed that Gorham was right and the Arches decision wrong, and was contemplating as a result the abandonment of his living and a return to lay communion. But A. B. saw that the fact that a decision was in his view right did not affect the question whether it was valid or binding. He begged his reader to keep his living, to maintain his own doctrine unless and until he came round of his own accord to accept what A. B. regarded as a better one. Why? Because the State has no power in matters of doctrine and Sir Herbert Jenner Fust is not an expert. He rejoices, he says, in Fust's decision in the same way that a man accused of mystical high-flown ideas would rejoice when he found that a farmer agreed with him. Not because the farmer was an expert, but because he was not. Fust was a lawyer, not a theologian. It was to be presumed that he was a man of good general intelligence.

He had examined the arguments of both sides carefully, therefore it was pleasant to know that he had endorsed one's own view. But the judgment had no authority at all. The author of this letter therefore was one of the few who was able, when the Arches decision was surprisingly reversed by the Privy Council, to maintain a perfectly consistent attitude to both decisions.

The same letter indicates with great insight why the circumstances of the case made the tactical position of his own and Phillpott's party so weak. The British public, as he says, do not like to see a bishop taking a rigid stand on ancient formularies, and they usually favour a rebel against any authority short of the Crown. But he said that if the issue would be clearly explained to them, shorn of these accidental features (for it might just as well have been a bishop who held Gorham's views and a clergyman who held Phillpotts's), the Christian public would not consent to throw over baptismal regeneration and accept the corollary, that baptised infants were or might be children of Satan. This analysis made clear an irony that was hidden from the majority of the public. It was the angry, over-bearing bishop who maintained a doctrine enshrining the idea of God's universal mercy. It was the brave clergyman threatened with loss of livelihood and resisting authority for conscience sake who proclaimed the severity of God's inscrutable judgment upon infants.

As the author of this pamphlet clearly saw, Phillpotts's position, whatever its logical strength, was tactically very weak. Public opinion was always watchful against Rome. And the later stages of the case coincided in time with the "Papal aggression" scare which followed the establishment by Pius IX of a new hierarchy in England. Few High Churchmen were so little likely to be influenced by Rome as Phillpotts. He had been born in 1778, at a time when the

Roman Church in England was numerically weak, when conversions to it were rare. He had in his youth engaged in anti-Roman controversy, but in the style of a man rebuking intellectual error, not at all with a view to guarding against a present danger. He was insular and oblivious of all continental influences whether religious, cultural, or political. But High Churchmen are always apt to seem to Protestant eyes much nearer to Rome than they really are. Moreover, it was bad luck from Phillpotts's point of view, that Badeley, a lawyer who represented him before the Privy Council, should have later become a convert to Rome. The principle of guilt by association, though foreign to English law, has a time-honoured place in our controversy. And many people must have read with fascinated horror propaganda designed to prove that Phillpotts was a disguised agent of the Pope. Evidence like this strongly suggested that public opinion, by a majority, was against Phillpotts. Moreover, from the legal point of view, Phillpotts appeared as the accuser and Gorham as the defendant. The legal system has a laudable and excellent bias in favour of the defendant in doubtful cases. The theological view, which would consider Gorham as the challenger or aggressor against agreed and traditional formulas, naturally made no appeal to secular judges. In a doubtful case it is better to err in favour of the weak than of the powerful. All these honourable considerations and many others may have played a part in the final decision. But all these considerations were alike irrelevant to a purely theological issue. The Gorham case made many people realise for the first time that, whenever secular courts are asked to decide religious questions, such human and legal considerations are liable to prevent the judges from reaching an objective decision.

And to reinforce the doubts thus aroused, there arose for the first time in many minds the simple long-neglected question: " Has the Crown any right to decide questions of doctrine? " To this question there came few coherent answers; and such answers as there were, were based on expediency rather than on principle.

It might seem that the concurrence of the archbishops preserved the decision of the Privy Council from any taint of Erastianism or of tyranny. But in the eyes of Gorham's opponents, of Manning, Gladstone and Pusey for instance, the agreement of the archbishops only made things worse. Instead of protesting they had acquiesced in a state-controlled Christianity and a state-tailored doctrine. The archbishops sitting meekly beside the Privy Council seemed to many High Churchmen like a living tableau of the Church Enchained.

From 1850 onwards it was clear that the State claimed supremacy in doctrine as well as discipline and that, for the time being at any rate, the leaders of the Church would not seriously contest the claim. The consequences were far-reaching. The High Church was of course the hardest hit at the moment. But Low Churchmen also might well feel apprehensive when they considered that their victory in the Gorham case was fortuitous, and that the State, once its right to decide was conceded, would probably proceed in due course to declare some portion of the creed particularly dear to them to be as inessential as baptismal regeneration. This would actually happen, as we shall see, some ten years later in the case of *Essays and Reviews*.

But there were others to whom the Gorham judgment brought only encouragement. The Broad Church school were delighted both at the actual decision of the Privy Council and because an organ of the State had decisively over-ridden what they considered the narrow reactionary judgment of the bishops and the meaningless attempt to test orthodoxy by ancient creeds and formulas. Dean

Stanley had plainly declared in an article in the *Edinburgh Review* what the Broad Church considered the crucial issue of the case. " Was the Church of England to be a national Church or was it to be a sect? " What better proof could there be of the Church's national character than this? It had been shown that the ultimate ruler of the Church was exactly the same as that of the State— the Queen, acting of course constitutionally through her ministers and through the courts.

Roman Catholics were encouraged not only because the Gorham case helped to provide them with some notable recruits, but because the Gorham judgment tended to confirm what they had always thought about the Church of England. They had always maintained that it was Erastian in its constitution, and that it had never effectively exorcised the secular control claimed by Henry VIII. Here was Queen Victoria, acting no doubt in a much milder fashion than Henry VIII, but acting on precisely the same assumption, that the State was entitled to dictate to the Church. *Semper eadem.*

The agnostic intellectuals were naturally somewhat more detached than the parties just mentioned from a mere struggle between rival Christian doctrines. But they were encouraged to reflect that the supporters of religion were worried and divided, that the theoretically Christian character of the State, though no doubt deplorable in principle, was continually hampering the freedom of Christians. They meanwhile were left alone to pursue in peaceful confidence their task of building up the vast structure of certain secular knowledge and of refuting for the satisfaction of all future ages the superstitions which had for so long been interwoven with the moral truths of the Gospel.

CHAPTER FOUR

The Doctrinal Crisis

IN 1860 a volume was published which at once attracted the attention of all those whose minds were exercised about the doctrinal position of the Church of England. There were seven contributors to the book; Mark Pattison, Benjamin Jowett, and Professor Baden-Powell were noted Oxford figures; Frederick Temple, later Archbishop of Canterbury, was headmaster of Rugby, while Professor Rowland Williams, H. B. Wilson, and C. W. Goodwin were less eminent but still scholarly contributors. All were men of weight in the Church of England, and all except Goodwin were clergymen. Many people on reading the book instinctively felt that it was disloyal to the Church, but some readers found it hard to say just where the error lay, and exactly what Anglican doctrines were contravened. Had the authors contravened the Articles? Could a charge be brought home against any of them? Eventually, after much heart-searching and disagreement about the best way of deciding these questions, Williams was accused before the Court of Arches for his article on biblical criticism, and Wilson for his article on the national Church. They were found guilty, suspended, and later, on appeal, acquitted by the Privy Council. A verdict in one court was of no avail if it was to be overturned in another. Many people were led to think very seriously about the whole doctrinal position. Hamilton, Bishop of Salisbury, in a charge, made this

temperate statement of the case: " However comprehensive
may be the limits within which our tolerant Church allows
her clergy to exercise their ministry, those limits must
exist somewhere." But what were these limits, and how
were those who transgressed them to be punished?
Or were there perhaps in practice no limits at all?
There was no obvious or agreed answer to any of these
questions.

It might be supposed from all this that *Essays and Reviews*
was a vague and elusive book, but this is true only in one
sense and not in another. The authors were men of forceful
mind, and their writings were only vague when they were
so deliberately. They did not wish to be precise about
dogmatic definitions, and it would be impossible to extract
a complete religious system from the volume. But in another
sense the book was the reverse of vague. Several of the
authors were men of unusual personal force. Baden-
Powell was as fond of a knock-me-down argument as
Samuel Johnson. Jowett could never have attained his
unique personal influence on that most intractable of bodies,
the University of Oxford, without rare force of character.
If the seven were inclined to be hesitant in their assertions,
it was not because they lacked decisiveness, but in order that
they might be all the more vehement in their denials. You
could not fail to gather from the book that almost every
religious system so far professed on earth was palpably
mistaken. Jowett rejected the allegorical interpretation of
the Bible, Baden-Powell, writing on the evidences of
Christianity, described it as self-evident that faith could not
be a virtue or have merit, for no man could help his beliefs.
Rowland Williams dismissed altogether the idea of prophecy
in the Bible. Frederick Temple was very severe on Mosaic
eating laws. In place of the many dogmas of earlier faiths
the essayists set up one of their own. They were convinced

that the rapid decline and disappearance of dogma was both inevitable and desirable. The ultimate aims of the authors might be doubtful, for Utopias are always hard to picture; but the men who write about Utopias generally have very decided opinions. The book has all the theoretical clarity and all the imaginative vagueness of a liberalism that was still a conscious adventure, still struggling to find proper expression.

Some of the points which excited opposition may seem slight enough to-day. The chronology and authorship of Genesis, for instance, are questions of greater historical interest than theological importance. Yet nearly everyone who was interested in religious controversy at all, felt that the publication of these essays marked a crisis in the Church of England. For they raised the question, is religion given to man, or made by man? Ought religious beliefs and forms to adapt themselves to men and to change in time, or ought men to adapt themselves to religion? These questions were represented in a number of different ways by the essayists, but it was always essentially the same issue. The essayist said over and over again that religious beliefs were made by man and for man and that they had no divine authority. Temple implied this when he spoke of the Mosaic law; Baden-Powell when he spoke of faith. Wilson proclaimed that a national Church must correspond to the national character, that unpopular or troublesome doctrines must be discarded. All seven writers spoke as if Christianity came naturally to the man of reasonable education and culture. They all considered its moral code, instead of being as Christians had always supposed, difficult, exacting, and contrary at many points to natural instincts, to be only a sublime statement of the normal feelings of a gentleman. This opinion had two important consequences. It tended to make them reject any part of the traditional moral code

64

which seemed not to conform to the rule they had imposed on it. It tended to limit the possession of a truly Christian conscience to those who had received a similar moral and intellectual training to themselves. The inhabitant of an East End slum might or might not possess the conscience of a Christian as the idea had been previously understood. But it was certain that he did not possess the instincts of a gentleman. And then, what happened when one's gaze wandered outside Europe? What about the Hindus, to whom the burning of widows seemed as clearly and self-evidently right as giving a chair to a lady seemed to Jowett and Temple? If Christian ethics are merely the product of normal good feelings, then the ethics of the heathen, instead of being merely mistaken, become positively diabolical. Underrating perhaps the distinctiveness of the Christian ethical system, and the difficulty of conforming to it, they were driven in logic to take a terribly severe view of all those millions who led their lives on a totally different plan. Logic, yes; but they were kind-hearted men, and were reluctant to take this last step. It is noticeable that whenever the heathen makes a momentary appearance in *Essays and Reviews* the subject is hastily changed.

Bishop Wilberforce said of *Essays and Reviews*: " Nor in this system is all former belief to be cast away at the rude assault of an avowed infidelity; on the contrary it is to be treated with the utmost tenderness. It is not even stated to be false; in a certain sense, it, too, is allowed to be true; for there is nothing which is wholly true or wholly false. It is but one phase of the true—an imperfect, childish, almost infantine phase, if you will; to be cherished in remembrance like the ornaments or the delights of childhood, only not to be rested in by men; to be put away and looked back upon, as an early form which, as soon as the spirit which had of old breathed through them, revealed itself in a rosy light, dissolved like the frost-work of the morning beneath the full sunlight of noon."

It is in this sense then, a profoundly important one, that we can give an affirmative answer to the question " Did all the essayists mean the same thing? " In spite of their many differences of opinion, they all meant that Christianity at its best was the fine flower of natural religion, that doctrine was by nature variable, and that no plenary, unchanging revelation had ever been vouchsafed to men.

We have now to consider the impact of such a system upon the England of 1860. Throughout the 1840's and 1850's there was a widespread but indefinite feeling that religion was being undermined. In one sense at least the feeling was justified; increasing numbers of educated people were joining the Roman Catholic church or abandoning religion altogether. Both the Roman and the agnostic influence were felt to be foreign; one located, a traditional and well-known enemy, in Rome, the other, more tentatively associated with Germany. The German liberal theology and the German biblical criticism affected myriads, more than ever read them. They became for many people a special enemy and a hidden fear. On the other side the debacle in Oxford in 1845 and the restoration of the Roman Catholic bishops in 1850 suggested that the old enemy had learnt new tactics. The supporters of Protestantism, which had had almost a monopoly not only of material privilege but of intellectual tradition for so long, felt hemmed in. Their majority seemed to be slipping away. Worse still, their certitudes might follow. Many felt that it was the moment for the strong hand, for firm doctrinal pronouncements by the bishops or by the lay courts. People were jumpy; they felt touchy about small points of ceremonial. There was a feeling that if only the agnostic enemy would submit to a pitched battle instead of all these isolated raids, a

66

real victory might be attained. The emotional climate of the fifties was that of the hour before zero hour.

In the circumstances, then, it is not surprising if there was a certain carelessness about the identification of enemies. 1860 was a bad moment to produce a book deprecating the importance of the Bible and Church. *Essays and Reviews* consisted of seven long essays, by seven different authors, all except one clergymen of the Church of England. In other circumstances this might have seemed a guarantee of orthodoxy. But in the suspicious, disunited state of the Anglican Church, it was the reverse. The enemies within the gates seemed both more numerous and more dangerous than those without. The nostalgic longing on the part of the High Church party for real Episcopal authority coalesced with a nostalgic longing in the Evangelicals for a church really governed by the infallible words of Scripture. *Essays and Reviews* offended both parties by their easy assumption that creeds and gospels and liturgies are only words, which ought to change as conditions change. There was a feeling that, while it might not be certain just where the line ought to be drawn, at any rate it ought to be drawn very firmly indeed.

Then there was a feeling that the seven men taken together were far too important to be ignored. One could not write off as a mere clique Jowett, Master of Balliol, Frederick Temple, headmaster of Rugby, Mark Pattison, a distinguished Oxford figure. These were famous men. While of the others, H. B. Wilson and Baden-Powell were both Oxford professors, and Charles Goodwin was the brother of a bishop, a former fellow of a Cambridge college, and a legal and literary figure of some distinction. The range of their learning was considerable. Jowett was professor of Greek, Wilson of Anglo-Saxon, Williams of Hebrew, and Baden-Powell of geometry; Pattison was expert in some periods of English history. But what after all did *Essays and Reviews* inculcate?

Had it a policy and an aim? The authors themselves denied a corporate responsibility. They stated that they had not seen each others' contributions before the book went to press. A prefatory note to the volume stated that responsibility for each contribution was personal and not shared. Some people felt that, while this statement was no doubt true, it was perhaps a little disingenuous. They knew each others' views; they knew the book might raise a storm. They decided that each should bear his own burden of public blame.

General opinion, with that rough and ready insensitive justice which often characterises it, refused to accept their contention of separate responsibility. The essays, argued the ordinary reader, are all in one volume, they all tend the same way, the authors know each other pretty well. They are all in it together. The crucial question was, did the essays all tend the same way? A brisk and memorable answer to this question awarded the authors the joint title of *Septem contra Christum*. It is hard to tell how general this estimate was, for it is the kind of phrase which is repeated as a *bon mot* by many who do not really agree with it, by some who have no interest in religious questions at all, and by some who make it their business to encourage a stand-up fight between various factions in the Church.

Perhaps the most obvious difference between the contributors lay in their temperament and tone of speaking. While Jowett, Pattison and Baden-Powell were all natural controversialists, Temple was a man of peace though also a man of firm character, capable of resenting bitterly anything that he considered suggestive of treachery. The tone of a theological publication quite as much as its doctrinal implications (which few will pursue to their logical conclusion) determines the public's reaction. Temple's essay was quiet and restrained and certainly more in accordance with traditional ideas than the writings of many who never had to suffer under a public outcry. Temple was a little unhappy about some of the other contributions when he saw them, apparently for the first time, in print. Friends urged him to dissociate himself from the other essayists; he would perhaps have liked to do this, and some years later when the dispute had died down, and when he was nominated to the bishopric of Exeter, he did disown opinions contained in the book. But he seems to have felt that to disown them at the time, even if it would have been honest, as he was in no way responsible for the others, would have seemed disloyal and cowardly. In Temple we see a man publicly pilloried for theological opinions which he did not hold but which his honour forbade him to repudiate publicly. This painful position naturally made him somewhat touchy in his private dealings with his friends.

The party of the accusers was as little united as that of the essayists themselves. Wilberforce, Bishop of Oxford, who disapproved of all seven essays, wished to avoid legal proceedings against any, while Tait, Bishop of London, who disapproved of most, wished to exonerate Temple and Jowett. But Tait's attitude was changeable, and his indecision makes an interesting contrast with Temple's violent criticism of Tait as a friend who had failed him. As so often in this period all the certainty and the offensive power was to be found in the younger men, in subordinate ecclesiastical positions, and belonging to an isolated group; the heart-searching and uncertainty was on the side of the official authorities. At first, it seems, Tait expressed in private to Jowett a qualified approval of the volume, then he added his signature to a letter of the Archbishop of Canterbury which totally condemned it. Finally, acting with the two archbishops as assessor to the Judicial Committee of the Privy Council, he voted with the lay majority against both the archbishops in favour of acquitting Williams and Wilson. Before this last change he received a letter from Temple which included this angry prophecy: "You will not keep your friends if you compel them to feel that in every crisis of life they must be on their guard against trusting you." Strange for a bishop to receive such a letter from a clergyman, but the controversies sometimes upset all the normal barriers and hierarchies. A clergyman might suddenly become a national figure; a bishop might find himself helpless.

It is interesting to contrast *Essays and Reviews* with some of the numerous replies and rebuttals which it aroused. Perhaps the most important of these was the volume entitled *Aids to Faith*, a work made up of contributions from scholars —men on the whole of the same general background and education as the essayists. We notice first of all that *Aids to Faith* is a much more modest book than *Essays and Reviews*. It argues in favour of the creeds, in favour of biblical inspiration, and in general for a traditional Anglican conception of Christianity. Thus it supports a system, which, if not exactly well defined, is at least much clearer and more coherent than that advocated by the essayists. Partly for this reason, perhaps, it does not shout so loud.

Yet the authors of *Aids to Faith* were not altogether a happy alliance. Just as Temple might regret provocative remarks by Williams or Baden-Powell, so might Professors Rawlinson and Brown be doubtful about each other's contributions to *Aids to Faith*. They did not really agree about biblical inspiration, though they were agreed in deploring what the essayists had said of it. Professor Rawlinson, without explaining why, without even giving any real authority, laid great stress on the supposed chronology of the Old Testament, and therefore rejected certain geological evidence. Professor Brown took a much less rigid view, and suggested (though without definitely committing himself to the view) that inspiration means no more than general help and guidance.

Such discrepancies were really symptomatic of the whole situation. The religious conflicts of the Victorian age were fought out by an ill-assorted army. A man might be nearer in spirit to his enemy than to his friend.

I I

There was one school of thought which might have been expected to be more constant in condemnation of *Essays and Reviews*—the school of Pusey. Pusey did indeed describe the final judgment of the Privy Council allowing the appeal of Williams and Wilson, as miserable and soul-destroying. But it is doubtful whether the feelings of his followers, or even his own, were really as strong as this phrase would suggest. The real crisis, the real cross-roads for these men, had come in 1850 with the Gorham case. Whereas the issues in *Essays and Reviews* were ill-defined, in the Gorham case they had been crystal. The authors of *Essays and Reviews* were not reckless men. They suggested more than they stated, and it was more their manner than their doctrine that gave offence. But the Gorham case, from the High Church point of view, was clear. Gorham, a man of perfect lucidity and considerable theological learning, denied the baptismal regeneration of infants; the courts held that he was within his rights as a clergyman of the Church of England in doing so. From 1850 may be dated the persistent, continuing contempt of High Churchmen for authority both civil and ecclesiastical in matters of faith. Whereas Newman had said that the lightest word of a bishop was a great thing to him, it is recorded that an Anglo-Catholic congress of the present century cheered at every mention of the Pope and laughed at every mention of the Archbishop of Canterbury. Newman's attitude seems consistent with the Tractarian position; the more modern attitude has usually seemed to outsiders either very puzzling or very irritating. In fact it is simply a necessity—a necessity which became clear once and for all at the time of the Gorham case, a decade before *Essays and Reviews*. Those who, like Manning, could not adopt such an attitude, left the Church of England after the Gorham judgment. Those who remained were forced to be contemptuous of authority if they were not to abandon their Church or their theological principles. As well blame a giraffe for having a long neck or a tortoise for its thick shell. Newman had dreamed of a Church becoming corporately conscious of apostolic origins and claims. By the 1860's the Anglo-Catholic was hardened, aware of being permanently in a minority, and his protests lacked the desperate urgency of former days. At each successive blow by bishops, courts, or Parliament against belief in the Catholic status of the Church of England since that time (and they have not been few) the true Anglo-Catholic has gritted his teeth, then grinned, and murmured " Same old story."

The history of the trial and the subsequent vindication of the essayists shows how misleading Anglican agitations can be. At first sight, Williams and Wilson seemed to be absolutely alone. The bishops, including the latitudinarian Thirlwall, had formally stated that, " we cannot understand how these opinions can be held consistently with an honest subscription to the formularies of the Church." The essayists had achieved the considerable feat of uniting High Church and Low Church opinion against them. Over ten thousand clergymen had signed an address of protest. Even Dean Stanley, whose instincts were entirely on their side, could only muster a partial and apologetic defence.

Nor could the essayists look for much support outside the establishment. Roman Catholics on the whole felt that it was not their quarrel. It is true that H. N. Oxenham, an Oxford convert to Rome, in a pamphlet of 1866 made this comment: " Of the three opinions which the courts refused to enforce, it must be remembered that one, as stated by them, is a heresy and one an open question. The Lutheran doctrine of imputed righteousness is expressly condemned by the Council of Trent; verbal inspiration has never been defined by the Church, and is probably held in our own day by very few theologians." This statement is interesting for several reasons, and partly because it reveals an outsider's attitude to a domestic Anglican quarrel. It shows too that the doctrines that went most against the grain with liberal theologians like the essayists were specifically Protestant. Manning in his usual forceful and orderly fashion gave, in his pamphlet *The Crown in Council*, a list of fundamental doctrines which the essayists denied. These included miracles, prophecy, and the Fall. But in fact the language of the essayists was hardly precise enough to come within the area of Manning's workmanlike categories. Nevertheless, Catholics could not be expected to concur with the essayists' strong distaste for the Christian centuries of the past.

The Nonconformists and the free-thinkers might have been expected to sympathise with liberal theologians ground down by authority. To-day when Anglican privileges are small, they probably would sympathise. But memories of tests and glebes and tithes and of Oxford inexorably forbidden to them were generally too strong for feelings of sympathy. The normal response of Nonconformist and agnostic was, "Here are we suffering, out of conscience, the loss of many privileges because we do not accept the teaching of the Prayer Book. Here are these men who

73

believe in it no more than we do, enjoying all the privileges of a clerical corporation, enjoying the favour of the State, and the generous, indeed luxurious endowments of past ages." Or as one pamphlet, significantly entitled *A Few Honest Words Addressed to Honest People by an Honest Man*, put it, " For a morsel of meat they are selling their birthright." That the views of the essayists, right or wrong, were really irreconcilable with traditional Anglicanism seems to have been common ground for almost everybody, except the Privy Council.

But of course the essayists' position was very much stronger than it looked. For one thing, the alliance of High Church and Low Church in defence of the inspired word of scripture was bound to be incomplete and temporary. We have already seen that the High Church had by now become hardened to unfavourable Episcopal and judicial decisions, putting their faith in a wide and ancient tradition which, they held, could implicitly overrule such judgments.

The Low Church was hardened in a different way. Scripture was the guide; the Anglican formularies clearly stated that Scripture was the guide. Yet the judges refused to judge the essayists by scripture. They deliberately said and repeated that they were not equal to such a task. Legal decision must be made according to the strict interpretation of words. General tendencies and intentions are excluded from legal discussion. To judge by the Bible would have been to open the door to a myriad of interpretations, each (in legal terms) as convincing as the next. The Low Church could feel with some reason that the *casus belli* had not arisen. If the judges had said that the essayists were writing in conformity with scripture it would have been a different matter. All the judgment proved was that the sixteenth century formularies were slippery and inadequate. But no one is more conscious than the Bible Christian of the slippery inadequacy of human formularies. In spite of fiery words neither the High nor Low Church was going to take so very much placating. Above all, time was on the side of the essayists; agitations die down; legal decisions can be reversed; gradually the prosecutors will take on, to unconcerned and nearly neutral millions, the guise of inquisitors. The idea of civil liberty was really, it is true, irrelevant. Beliefs demanded by the State are in a different category from beliefs demanded from the ministers of a voluntary religious organisation who, after all, have freely sworn to uphold them. Nevertheless, the idea of civil liberty will loom larger and larger in the kindly, inexact, liberal mind of a million citizens. The essayists, for the most part, looked out of firmly entrenched positions on a hostile but not really dangerous enemy. They were not easy to remove; they could afford to wait.

III

Of the seven contributors, Benjamin Jowett is still too famous a figure to need a very detailed biographical introduction. The poor London boy, the scholar, the professor of Greek, the Master of Balliol intellectually pre-eminent, the famous host, the friend of the great, all these facets of his life are familiar. His religious doctrine is more obscure; we do not know quite what to expect of a clergyman who proclaims that Voltaire has done more good than all the Fathers of the Church put together. But if Jowett's doctrines were indeterminate and shifting, the principle on which they were based was always the same. It was this: If Christianity seemed to be in conflict with the age, it must be altered to suit the age. He had a lofty vision of his own personal role in this reconstruction. It was with no sense of incongruity that he compared himself to Thomas à Kempis, and girded himself " to combine in a manual of piety religious fervour with perfect good sense and knowledge of the world . . . a book worthy of great religious genius."

Jowett wrote in a hopeful vein upon the interpretation of Scripture. The Bible, he insists, is not a difficult book; past ages erred in reading too much into it. What is required is the plain natural sense of the words. Unfortunately, no English version can provide this. Each of them was composed under the influence of mystical ideas which obscure the simplicity of the original. Those who do not know Greek must accept the authority of those who do. The cornerstone of his theory was that one word cannot have more than one sense. If this seems to-day a somewhat simple-minded attitude, we must make allowance for the fact that Jowett was not acquainted with the literary criticism of this century which has so often demonstrated the literary importance of ambiguity. Words to Jowett were as definite as chairs and tables, and he was confident that there was nothing in the Bible that he had not understood. Yet in spite of all this Jowett was unfortunate to find himself involved in the bitter struggle over *Essays and Reviews*. There was nothing obviously contrary to the Anglican formularies in his essay, for the simple reason that the subject matter was not the same. He wrote only as a scholar, which he was, and a man of literary sensibility, where his claim was more doubtful. He was loyal to his own conception of the English Church, which was similar to that of Stanley and the Latitudinarians. He had no wish to be a party man. His design was to be above party and to appeal to men of every theological school; But he found, like General de Gaulle, that to be of no party may seem more partisan than to belong to one.

Another interesting contributor was Mark Pattison. Born

in 1813, the son of a country clergyman, he had come to Oxford after a lonely boyhood, a diffident and impressionable young man. He was young for his age, and his natural ambition was quiescent for lack of fuel. In spite of his superior ability he felt like a child beside the sophisticated products of the great public schools. That a quiet, studious boy in the Oxford of the 1830's should be attracted by Newman and the tracts was not surprising, but the attraction was hesitant, delayed, and essentially superficial, as Newman himself early realised. It was not Newman's theological system that appealed to him, indeed he hardly comprehended it, but the moral strictness and the close self-examination which belonged to Newman's followers. Pattison exaggerated these elements in Newman's system out of all recognition. Such a superficial feeling for High Church principles was bound to fade. When it faded, Pattison was left with a dislike of all systems which conceived religion as supernatural and historical. He says in his memoirs that religion is a good servant but a bad master, and the religion which he came to profess was conveniently indefinite.

Pattison's contribution to *Essays and Reviews* seemed harmless enough. *Religious Thought in England, 1688-1750*—surely one could avoid doctrinal pitfalls there. In fact, little of the blame diverted against the volume was reserved for this contributor. Though it must be admitted that the presence of Pattison, a clergyman who distrusted all religion, in a volume designed to rebuild and renew the Church of England, needed some explaining. In fact the greater part of the essay merely analyses and describes the beliefs of a past period. But right at the end, there is a disturbing question—a question which was implicit in all sorts of different forms in the volume as a whole, a question which roused the various religious passions of the English people. The essay ends with these words: " Whoever would take the religious literature of the present day as a whole, and endeavour to make out clearly on what basis revelation is supposed by it to rest, whether on Authority, on the Inward Light, on Reason, on Self-evidencing Scripture, or on the combination of the four, on some of them, and in what proportions, would probably find that he had undertaken a perplexing but not altogether profitless inquiry." This is not the sort of remark that can be censured by ecclesiastical courts, but it is perhaps in some ways more disturbing to serious Anglicans than those that are.

It may seem strange to give pride of place to contributors who were not the subject of legal proceedings. But in fact the accused were not the most important contributors, nor were they, even in the eyes of the accusers, the most dangerous. The accusers were in a difficult position; they naturally wished to take as little risk as possible of an acquittal in the courts. Whom should they attack? Jowett hardly seemed to have dealt with matters covered in the Anglican formularies. Pattison's essay, though it contained searching and dangerous questions for Anglicans, was historical, not dogmatic. The contributions of Temple and Goodwin were comparatively unobjectionable. Most unfortunately Baden-Powell had suddenly died, so it was necessary to strike at the elusive Jowett and the dead Baden-Powell through their less dangerous and less famous colleagues.

How did Williams and Wilson give a handle for the attack? Williams had written on the delicate subject of biblical criticism, and had advocated the spread of German methods of treating it. He questioned the historical accuracy of Exodus, implied that St. Paul may have endorsed erroneous Old Testament accounts, and cast doubts on the whole idea of prophecy of the Saviour in the Old Testament. But some of his most disturbing comments were incidental, as when he referred to baptism as "degenerating into a magical form." It was not easy, however, to pin him down, most of his essay summarised the views of the critic Bunsen, and his own approval of these, though obvious, was seldom explicit.

Wilson, in his essay on the national Church, had proclaimed complete doctrinal freedom for the clergy. He reduced subscription to the Articles to a mere agreement to tolerate them. He showed that the legal obligation incurred by signing the Articles was extremely vague, and then added, " and in this case the strictly legal obligation is the measure of the moral one." This was particularly wounding to the orthodox, who were learning by bitter experience that the practical working of the law did not require any beliefs at all to be professed by the clergy. It was disturbing too to those who feared that the Church's doctrinal basis was slipping to be told that " As far as opinion privately entertained is concerned, the liberty of the English clergyman already appears to be complete."

As it turned out the hopes of the accusers were not fully realised. Even Williams and Wilson, after being condemned once, were to be acquitted on appeal. But it does not necessarily follow that the orthodox calculations were astray. It may be (and the events of the Colenso case a few years later tended to confirm this) that by now the Privy Council would not have condemned any Latitudinarian for heresy. For instance, one detects a distinct personal bias against the bishops in the Lord Chancellor's declaration upon the judgment condemning *Essays and Reviews* passed by Convocation. The drafting of this condemnation had been largely the work of Bishop Wilberforce, and everyone realised that the Lord Chancellor's comment was intended to refer to his popular nickname of " Soapy Sam." " The judgment," he said, " is simply a series of well-lubricated terms, a sentence so oily and saponaceous that no one could grasp it—like an eel it slips through your fingers, and is simply nothing."

It may be then that the orthodox policy was the most judicious possible in the circumstances. But what of the system that made such a policy necessary? Apparently, to get a man convicted of a theological offence, it was necessary to accuse someone else. This fact threw a curious light on the whole question of Anglican tests and formulas. One of the most important consequences of 1860 was to make many thoughtful people doubt whether Anglican loyalty could be tested at all. Perhaps it was not a matter of dogma; perhaps it was in some ways more like loyalty to a school—a matter of proper feeling, of a certain general community of outlook with one's fellows, a matter of solidarity and endurance in times of crisis. Many people felt that a loyalty of this kind was both more English and more in keeping with Anglican tradition than a loyalty subject to the tangible test of creed and canonical obedience, which seemed to some only an imitation of Rome. But of course you do not ask the courts to decide whether a man is loyal to his old school; it is not a matter on which legal discussion is useful. The logical conclusion of this view was that there could be no formal tests of Anglicanism, and that a man was an Anglican just so long as he himself thought he was. This was the view of Stanley, who was never afraid to follow his ideas to a logical conclusion. Tait, who was more hesitant, seemed on the whole to endorse it too.

But to Wilberforce or Pusey it represented a complete abdication by the bishops and the clergy of their inescapable duty, an abject selling of the past to the advancing forces of agnosticism and disintegration. One thing was clear; Stanley's view could easily be put into practice, but Wilberforce's was extremely difficult to apply. The formulas were ambiguous, the bishops were divided, the courts were unsympathetic, and Parliament took no notice. As the fifties and sixties wore on, all Anglicans who cared for a dogmatic version of Christianity, whether High Church or Low, were faced with a question that became always more difficult to answer. It was this: " can loyalty to the Church of England possibly be reduced to a formula and an oath? "

In the circumstances, the story of *Essays and Reviews* was bound to seem inconclusive. The trial of Williams and Wilson was certainly a strange affair, however conventional it may have seemed. To all appearances it was an ordinary court, with a learned and impartial judge, learned and courteous counsel. But behind this perfectly genuine façade lay a series of unanswered questions. First of all, by what right did the court judge? To answer that, one had to answer Pattison's question about the basis of revelation, that is to say, one had to decide upon the charges laid against the accused before one could decide whether the court had any right to sit.

The question to be decided was doctrinal authority. But who accepted the doctrinal authority of the court? The defendants did not because they thought it a restriction on freedom. The supporters of the prosecution did not because they for the most part distrusted lay judges responsible to the State in theological questions. Least of all did Lushington, the judge, accept his own authority. In the course of his judgment he pointed out that to judge a question of religious truth as if it were a question of law was an absurdity. Words are not used in the same way in doctrinal pronouncements as they are in legal documents. Lushington's judgment was, in effect, an appeal to the legislature to remove the burden of judging about heresy from the court over which he presided.

Then by what criteria was the case to be tried? By the

Prayer Book and Articles, said the judge. He set himself to decide if the writings of the accused were consistent with these. He specifically excluded all consideration of the Bible. No doubt this was the only practical course to take; it had respectable precedents. The whole thing, Lushington felt (and many agreed with him) was quite complicated enough without dragging in the Bible. Nobody knew what might not be found in the Bible; it might provide a colourable justification for all sorts of things. It contained massacres and the Song of Solomon. It spoke of the Four Horsemen and of the Mark of the Beast. It even contained Petrine texts and eucharistic discourses. Courts of law must come to a decision; the Bible had been disputed for century upon century. To reject the Bible for the purposes of legal judgment was by no means to decry it. Did not Newman say of it, " We have tried it and it disappoints; it disappoints, that most holy and blessed gift . . . because it is used for a purpose for which it was not given." ? No one could blame Lushington. But at the same time, it was very illogical. For the Articles and Prayer Book by which Lushington was to judge did not claim infallibility. They did clearly state that the Bible was the rule of faith. To judge by the Prayer Book and Articles alone, without reference to the Bible, was to judge dead against the Prayer Book and Articles. Pattison's simple-seeming query was very hard to answer.

It was perhaps no accident that in this case, as in most other doctrinal prosecutions of the time, the decision of one court was reversed by another. The law was powerless and indecisive, partly because it chose to be powerless and indecisive. Judges and Privy Council eagerly welcomed technicalities which might render it unnecessary to reach a decision. Whatever their personal opinions, they were administering a law in which, as lawyers, they found it hard to believe. They knew that any penalties they enforced were very likely to be ineffective. There is an unreal air about some of these legal proceedings. What, after all, were the Thirty-Nine Articles? Did they really represent the belief even of the most orthodox Churchman? A judge in an ecclesiastical case was apt to find himself in much the same position as the judge in *Trial by Jury*, administering law in which he could find no sense, but very much more sensitive about the anomaly of his position.

I V

We are sometimes assured that the issues in controversies such as this are trivial. Some thirty years later Randall Davidson, in his life of Tait, would express civilised astonishment that anyone should ever, even in the barbarous old 1860's, have been perturbed by such a harmless dove as *Essays and Reviews*. Learned and sympathetic writers of to-day concur in this judgment. But the heart knows its own bitterness. All that pain, doubt, fear and confusion were not based on nothing. Yet it is easy to see how the mistake arises. It is very natural, if not quite logical, to suppose that an inconclusive affair must also be trivial. Yet we all know that it is not always so; we remember how Sherlock Holmes drew Dr. Watson's attention to the fact that the dog did nothing in the night.

Essays and Reviews dealt with the foundations of religious authority. In asking the fundamental question, how can we know? the essayists rejected in turn all the recognised answers. Bible, Church, conscience, all were found wanting. Multitudes might protest against this nihilism, but Anglican tests and Anglican discipline were found to be ineffective against it. This was a discovery of the highest importance for the future. The inconclusiveness of the result constituted its importance.

We have seen that the non-Anglican public on the whole thought the essayists to be at odds with Anglican doctrine; they thought indeed that the disparity was obvious. The Privy Council ruled that the essayists were within the limits of conformity. This is not as paradoxical as it appears. It does not really, as might be supposed, tend to indicate public stupidity or prejudice on the one side, or absurd legal formalism on the other. For the public and the Privy Council both sat in judgment, but in different causes. The clash was much more apparent than real. Roman Catholics, Nonconformists and agnostics on the whole agreed that what was contained in *Essays and Reviews* was not historic Christianity. Diverse as their views of religion were, they were on the whole agreed on one vital point, Christianity was not a matter of common sense and the gentlemanly virtues. To the agnostic, Christianity was a primitive religion, containing among its doctrinal lumber useful or even perhaps precious moral truths, but relying for its appeal upon the dark, primitive, irrational instincts of man. Salvation by blood? A crude totemistic concept. Eternal life? A desperate attempt to escape from the unpleasant realities of this one. The Trinity? An incomprehensible mathematical fraud. The Incarnation? Sheer anthropomorphism. Nonconformists, various though their tenets were, were generally convinced that what was revealed to the spiritual man by the voice of God was infinitely exalted above the choicest speculation of the most acute intelligence working on merely rational principles. And they exalted faith far above works. Roman Catholics indeed held that reason was a precious tool in the search for faith and could establish certain vital truths on its own account. Nevertheless faith went altogether beyond reason's range. And then Catholics did not lay much stress on the gentlemanly virtues. Newman had shocked many gentlemanly instincts by saying that a lying, filthy Irish beggar-woman might be in a state of grace and go to heaven, while a sober, upright, conscientious English gentleman could not, merely on account of his sobriety and truthfulness, be necessarily pleasing to God if he lacked faith and charity.

These three conceptions of Christianity, very different though they were, had something in common. They all agreed in rejecting the essayists' implicit claim that Christianity was largely to be understood as a great civilising force, akin to benevolence, scholarship, and higher education. *Essays and Reviews* unlike the Oxford Movement itself represented a purely academic version of Christianity. Though many people in Oxford opposed it, the Oxford air was one in which it could flourish. It was not so persuasive everywhere else. The authors ignored, or failed to stress, human passions and frailty on the one hand, and on the other the desire for sanctity and the supernatural. One might gather from *Essays and Reviews* that it was easy to be good, but that it was unnecessary to be saintly. To agnostics, Nonconformists, and Catholics alike religion did not seem so simple.

It might seem then that the Privy Council went against public opinion in acquitting the essayists. But that is not necessarily so, for the Privy Council was not judging and could not attempt to judge the question in which public opinion was mainly interested. Public opinion asked, " Is this really Christianity? " The Privy Council in its official capacity could not answer or even ask this question. It could only ask, " Can these writings be reconciled with Prayer Book and Articles? " Public opinion could not be expected to penetrate very deeply into this complex issue. For non-Anglicans it was clearly a question irrelevant to their deepest convictions. But Anglicans too, as we have seen, had very generally come to doubt whether it was after all the question by which a man's orthodoxy must stand or fall.

Legal arguments had already in previous cases proved inconclusive and unsatisfactory. More and more Anglicans now felt that their loyalty was due to a living tradition and a liturgy rather than to a series of doctrinal statements. Many who felt that the essayists had much to answer for were still reluctant to see them condemned and disgraced by a charge based merely on the Articles. By 1860 very few people could maintain without hesitation that to question one or two of the Thirty-Nine Articles was equivalent to a subversion of the faith. Many Anglicans felt that to say this would only be to acquiesce in a legal fiction.

To agree to a serious penalty based on a legal fiction, public opinion would have to be roused to a very strong resentment. In the general uncertainty of Victorian intellectual life this resentment could not be sharp enough. Briefly then we may say that the essayists were never tried in a court of law for the offences of which thousands believed them to be guilty, and that two of them were tried for a different offence, most people were content with a verdict of "not proven." This may be regarded as a purely Anglican result. In the Roman Catholic system, where the real beliefs of the Church are formulated in precise statements, the two charges would have coalesced. He who denies an article of Catholic doctrine must inevitably be at odds with Catholic traditions. The same is true to some extent of the Free Churches, but to throw doubt on the Anglican formularies is itself part of the Anglican tradition. Many people felt that the lawyers were beating the air.

V

And so the inconclusiveness of the case was highly significant of the condition of the Church of England. The case
showed that the gap between the popular and the legal
standards of judgment about doctrine had grown too wide
to be bridged. The lawyers judged by the Articles, the
Anglo-Catholics mainly by the Creed. The great Protestant
mass of the population had two standards of judgment, the
Bible and private opinion. Each was an unanswerably
traditional Protestant standard; each was consecrated by
the martyrs of the Reformation and the heroes of the Civil
War. They had been assumed to be complementary. But
one was fixed and the other was variable. The essayists had
turned the traditional right of private judgment against the
traditional idea of the Bible, and against several leading
Protestant doctrines. Ecclesiastical authority was powerless
to act in the face of this manœuvre. Secular authority
refused to act. Lay opinion was mystified and deeply
divided. There seemed to be no remedy.

CHAPTER FIVE

The Crisis of Authority

THE BARE outline of the Colenso case can be simply stated. In 1862, when Robert Gray was Bishop of Cape Town and metropolitan, and J. W. Colenso was Bishop of Natal, Colenso published the first part of his book on the Pentateuch (or Books of Moses), succeeding parts of which appeared throughout the sixties and seventies. The book attempted to disprove the literal accuracy of these first books of the Old Testament. Colenso was summoned to appear before Gray on a charge of heresy, tried, declared to be deposed from his bishopric, and eventually excommunicated. On appeal, the Privy Council found that Gray had no power to try Colenso, because the Letters Patent from the Crown, which ascribed to Gray the right to hold such trials, had no validity in South African territory. In 1866 a judgment of the English courts known as the Romilly judgment confirmed Colenso in the temporal rights of his see where he remained until his death in 1883. Meanwhile, he had been condemned by the bench of bishops in England and a new bishop, Macrorie, was consecrated by Gray on their unanimous authority, to replace Colenso. For some 14 years there were two rival bishops sitting in Natal.

Such is the simple story, yet a startling one, and, in modern times unparalleled. Yet, when one considers the history and constitution of the Church of England, is it not perhaps surprising that such manifest opposition between Church and State has been so rare?

The Church of England is a State church. The twenty-first Article of religion says that general councils " may not be gathered together without the commandment and will of princes." The King is the supreme governor. But the Church also, by its episcopal order, its sacraments, and its creeds, identical with those recited and believed by Roman Catholics, and virtually identical with those of the Eastern Churches, implicitly claims continuity with the Catholic Church of the past. It is bound therefore to consider itself part of something catholic, that is, universal. For a long time the idea of a State church, controlled by a king, and the idea of a universal church had existed side by side in comparative peace. Few perhaps before 1830 had considered very carefully how they could be reconciled. But then the Oxford Movement had focused attention on the second proposition, continuity and universality of the Church, while the decisions in the Gorham case and in *Essays and Reviews* had clearly shown how much meaning was still contained in the words " the King is the supreme governor." If this supremacy was now exercised by the sovereign through the courts instead of directly, the practical difference was small.

Thus in the sixties the stage was neatly set for a *cause célèbre* which would raise the question, " how can civil frontiers and allegiance to States, affect spiritual truths? " The Colenso case was to show that a bishop of the Church of England had, legally, one set of rights and duties in England and another in South Africa. People asked themselves if this was logical; and how did it affect that implicit claim to be catholic, universal?

Again, before the nineteenth century, Anglicans, apart from few travellers, had generally lived in territories owing civil allegiance to the British crown. What was to happen if the

Church desired to spread beyond these boundaries? Or if these boundaries were to contract? If a colony became a dominion, the King in Parliament would cease to legislate for it in secular matters. Did this mean that in a dominion the ultimate legal authority in church affairs reverted to the bishops? Or, paradoxically, did a secular monarch, having surrendered his secular powers in South Africa, retain unimpaired his spiritual authority, which had originally derived solely from the now abandoned secular power? It was no use looking at sixteenth century formulas for answer to questions like these. The events of the Colenso case would not clearly answer them, but would show that they were both perplexing and urgent, and that disagreement upon them could bring schism and hatred into a new colonial church. The schism has so far lasted for nearly a century; the hatred, thanks to the fundamental generosity of the protagonists, would soon diminish and almost disappear.

From one point of view, then, the Colenso case arose because of the technical and legal difficulties of a Church which had claimed as an inheritance from the undivided Church the organisation of a few ecclesiastical provinces only, as it tried to transform itself into a world-wide society. From another, it showed the tension so long muted and even forgotten between the Catholic (and Anglican) idea of church government by bishops, the Protestant (and Anglican) idea of the supremacy of private judgment in religion, and the peculiarly Anglican idea of church government by kings. The question was made more searching and dangerous because it was a bishop who was accused of undermining the faith of the Church. Who ought to uphold the Church's faith in the Bible if not a bishop? But on the other hand, who had a better right than a bishop to reinterpret the Bible in the light of modern thought?

I I

Colenso was the son of a petty civil servant, whom he later had to support financially. He had to win scholarships to educate himself, and it was the culmination of long and creditable efforts when he became a fellow of St. John's College, Cambridge. His name, which was later to strike some of his enemies as suspiciously un-English, was really Cornish; and he grew up in an environment lacking in strong Anglican traditions—a county where Nonconformists were numerous and High Churchmen almost unknown. His early letters show that he was unaware of any fundamental distinction between Church and Chapel. Some of his relatives were Chapel, and he hesitated for some time between the calling of an Anglican and a Free Church pastor. His decision was eventually made on practical rather than on doctrinal grounds. He considered that an Anglican parson had greater " opportunities for usefulness " and greater independence. The factor decisive to his mind seems to be contained in a sentence full of ironic and perhaps prophetic force. " When once" he wrote, " the Church [i.e. Anglican] minister is settled in his church, unless guilty of some heinous dereliction, he cannot be expelled." One does not know whether to applaud the insight of this remark, or to regard it, taken with the sequel, as one more instance of the uncertainty of human affairs. For certainly Colenso was never false to his own conception of duty, never self-seeking, never lacking in zeal. His character was simple and attractive; he had a real sense of the human dignity of the Zulus; he was capable of consecrating his whole life to a cause. Yet he was solemnly deposed of his bishopric with the unanimous consent of the other bishops. On the other hand, and here his foresight was justified, he was never expelled from his diocese, never prevented from exercising his episcopal functions, and he remained for many years after sentence had been passed the Bishop of Natal, recognised by the Crown, ministering to a devoted congregation.

If he had remained in England, he might have lived a calm and useful life, respected by all; he would have associated with people like himself. His religion, clean, instinctive, undogmatic and morally exacting, was the religion of millions of his countrymen. The Fatherhood of God, the authority of conscience, the fundamental goodness of human nature, these were the pillars of his simple creed. He was impatient with theological subtleties.

Colonial bishoprics were not greatly sought after at this time. A man had to cut himself off, more than was necessary at a later date, from English ties. Colenso with his conscientious zeal, willingness to sacrifice himself, and incisive, if not brilliant mind, seemed an excellent choice. People may have wondered what effect he would have on the Zulus, but perhaps no one bothered to speculate what effect the Zulus might have on him, and through him on the whole Anglican Church.

A prolonged residence among a people strange to him is always likely to alter a man's conception of religion, especially if his religion is undogmatic. For undogmatic religion is based on conscience, instinct and a general idea of the fitness of things, and the fitness of things may not seem such a clear guide among the Zulus as it does in London. A religion based upon dogma can be accepted (and rejected) by men of every race. But religious instincts everywhere vary and religion based upon them is not easily transplanted into an alien culture. Colenso was soon troubled with conscience by the problem of Zulu polygamy. If converts were forced to abandon the practice forthwith serious

social consequences followed. There would be bands of
cast-off uncared-for women who had committed no offence
against the customs of their own country. Colenso therefore wrote a pamphlet suggesting that doctrine which led
to this result must be over-harsh, and inapplicable in its
full rigour to African communities. It is safe to say that if
he had remained in London Colenso would not have
written a pamphlet in defence of polygamy.

Nor in all probability would he have worried about the
credibility of the Old Testament. But the Zulus wanted to
know a great many things, and in the words of Colenso's
own account they asked him: " is all that true? Do you
really believe that all this happened thus,—that all the beasts,
and birds, and creeping things upon the earth, large and
small, from hot countries and cold, came thus by pairs and
entered in the ark with Noah? And did Noah gather food
for them *all*, for the beasts and birds of prey, as well as the
rest?" In the face of these naïve yet searching questions,
" My heart answered " he said, " in the words of the
Prophet, ' Shall a man speak lies in the Name of the Lord? '
Zech. xii.3. I dared not do so." It is worth noting that at
this crucial moment he turned to a biblical text for inspiration and guidance. An Evangelical upbringing had made
him a Bible Christian and this is what in spirit he always
remained. When he had ceased to believe in its truth he
interpreted the Bible with just the same literalness, just the
same demand for an infallible utterance in every sentence
as the Evangelical party had done in his youth. So it came
about that in attacking the Old Testament, Colenso differed
from the authors of *Essays and Reviews* in that he saw Genesis
and the succeeding books as *pure history*, with no symbolical
elements whatsoever. In this, of course, he was going against
the main streams of theology. The orthodox were entitled
to respond that while Colenso might have approved of the

Bible inadequate as pure history, no one else need suppose that that was what it was intended to be. But few made this distinction; most people felt as Colenso himself did, that the question was simple. The Bible had been attacked; it must be defended.

Colenso was in some ways ill-prepared for the ordeal to which the Zulus had exposed him. For he was one of those men who naturally regard every problem as a simple one. His mind was lucid, but lacking in finesse. He was a mathematician, and in mathematics the criteria of accuracy are precise. If Colenso's voluminous books of biblical criticism do not perhaps give a satisfying account of the Bible as a source of religious authority, they do answer the question, what is the value of the Bible as a mathematical treatise? The answer to this question was prolonged, but never doubtful. How many men, women, and children could be accommodated within the Temple? Colenso worked out the measurements, estimated the number of cubic feet required by each person, and found that the total was different from the stated number of the Children of Israel. F. D. Maurice, once his friend, now compelled to differ from him, said epigrammatically but not unfairly, " His idea of history is that it is a branch of arithmetic."

Biblical criticism raises complex questions about the nature of meaning. Medieval theologians had found four different levels of meaning in the Bible. Indeed, in considering any work cast in a literary form, the concepts of truth and accuracy need to be very carefully analysed. But Colenso thought that if even the numbers were wrong, the rest must be unreliable. Numbers, he thought, were plain and could not be argued against. " If my conclusions," he wrote, " indeed, were only *speculations*, if they were only matters of higher or lower *probability*, I feel that I should have no right to express them at all in this way, and thus, it may be, disturb

94

painfully the faith of many. But the main result of my examination of the Pentateuch,—viz. that the narrative, whatever may be its value and meaning, cannot be regarded as historically true,—is not—unless I greatly deceive myself—a doubtful matter of speculation at all; it is a simple question of *facts*." But the very fact that he chose such mundane, mechanical criteria was an added offence to many who were solely concerned with the spiritual value of the Old Testament. As Maurice wrote: "To have a quantity of criticism about the dung in the Jewish camp, and the division of a hare's foot, thrown in my face, when I was satisfied that the Jewish history had been the mightiest witness to the people for a living God against the dead dogmas of priests, was more shocking to me than I can describe."

III

Robert Gray, on his appointment to the see of Cape Town, had acquired an undefined office of metropolitan, upon which so much of the controversy was to turn. It was laid down that he was to have the same rights over the bishops of his province as the Archbishop of Canterbury had over the English bishops. But it soon became clear that there were many different views, none fully authoritative, about the nature of those rights.

Himself an Etonian, the son of a bishop, Gray's mind had been formed in a purely Anglican atmosphere. A nervous, bookish, ungregarious boy, loneliness had tended to make him ignorant of the views of others, while his natural tendency to self-dramatisation made him overlook their importance when they were known. As the case proceeded his self-dramatisation increased. When his judgment on

Colenso was about to be considered by the Privy Council, he wrote to his son (17th February, 1865): "I may at any moment be plunged into a struggle, the issue of which it is impossible to foresee, but which may end in my ruin and death." It is very disagreeable, no doubt, and very expensive, to appear before the Privy Council, but it is not quite so bad as that. If Colenso's upbringing led him to think of the Church of England as just a larger and more efficient Protestant sect, Gray's upbringing led him to ignore the part played by the Protestant sects in the religious life of the nation, and by Protestant traditions in the formation of the Church of England. He was a High Churchman, but one curiously dissimilar in outlook from the leaders of the Oxford Movement. For the keynote of the Oxford policy was battle. Nobody knew better than Newman, comparing himself in 1833 to Achilles returning to the fray, ("You shall know the difference now that I am back again") or than Hurrell Froude proclaiming his intention to dictate to the bishops, how strong was Protestant feeling within the Church. But Gray invariably overestimated the strength of his own party and was invariably disappointed. Far from England and from theological controversy (until chance and Colenso's book brought South Africa into the limelight), this rather unobservant man was able to maintain his idea that everybody in the Church of England thought as he did himself upon theological questions. He regarded Colenso as a monstrous portent. But Colenso, after all, was not the first of the Latitudinarian bishops.

By what standard was he to judge Colenso, and how was he to determine the limits of that dubious and brittle power, coupled with heavy responsibility, which was vested in him as metropolitan? Colenso's book was a challenge to him to say how far the Old Testament was to be regarded as a pure historical record, and how far it was permissible to regard it instead as a theological or symbolical statement. But Gray did not take up this challenge; perhaps he did not see it. He answered in the most general but definite terms that the Bible was true (in a sense not specified) and must not be questioned. This implied or seemed to imply literal historical accuracy. Part of the irony of the Colenso case was that metropolitan and subordinate, persecutor and persecuted, one apparently traditional, the other apparently a reckless innovator, were agreed, in combined and unconscious opposition to traditional theology, and the interpretation of St. Augustine and the Fathers, that the Bible could only be discussed if it were regarded in all its parts as a historical account and nothing more. The traditional Bible, with its metaphors, its prophecies, its parables, and all its complex interpretation disappeared from view. For one it was literally true, for the other it was literally false.

Gray was continually using phrases like this: "What the Catholic Church, while yet one, during the first thousand years of her history, under the Spirit's guidance in her great councils declared to be . . . the true faith, that is the true faith." In fact, Gray and Colenso were united in holding a most untraditional view. In any case, Gray's principle of appeal to the universal consent of antiquity was a difficult one to maintain as being a distinctively Anglican principle. As Colenso pointed out, the twenty-first Article of Religion said that Councils might err.

Both men saw the question as a fundamentally simple one. Colenso knew he was right because his arithmetic had proved it; if he had found the truth it was his duty to proclaim it, and there could be no higher duty. Gray knew he was right because the Bible was part of the faith which he and Colenso had sworn to uphold. Neither man was influenced by personal spite; indeed until they were driven apart by a sense of duty and overriding loyalty to truth, they were friends. Each respected the other's determination and sense of duty; each realised that the other was trying to be just, even if he was obviously in the wrong. Each was engaging in a dangerous battle, risking unpopularity and perhaps deposition. It would have been two remarkable men who did not become a little heated and hasty in the course of the struggle. In many ways similar in character, the courage and tenacity of each shone brighter as their conflict grew more bitter. Each was true to his conscience; they were " united in the strife which divided them."

I V

Moreover it is hard to say that either was thoroughly in the wrong, in terms of the abiding convictions and policies of the Church of England. It was a conflict between the authority of the Bible and private judgment. But the Church of England believes in both these principles. It was a battle between the authority of the bishops and the power of the State over the bishops. The Church of England accepts both. Throughout the Victorian controversies one is driven to wonder, not that the disputes were so violent, but that they were so long delayed; that tensions implicit in the very nature of Anglicanism had been ignored for so long.

The tension between the Anglican belief in the Bible and the Anglican belief in private judgment was neatly pointed out by Colenso in the preface to his second volume. He quoted Tait, Bishop of London, who had said: " As to free inquiry, what shall we do with it? Shall we frown upon it, denounce it, try to stifle it? This will do no good, even if it be right. But after all we are Protestants. We have been accustomed to speak a good deal of the right and duty of private judgment. It was *by the exercise of this right, and the discharge of this duty*, that our fathers freed their and our souls from Rome's time-honoured falsehoods." " But," Colenso went on, " if anyone actually exercised this right of private judgment, he knows that, for arriving at any conclusions on certain points of Biblical criticism, which contradict the notions of our forefathers, living in days of comparative darkness and ignorance in respect of all matters of scientific research, he may be dragged into the Court of Arches, and there by legal process be forcibly ejected, or, if not ejected, at least suspended from his living and saddled for life with a crushing weight of debt, at the instance, it may be, of some good, easy brother, who never, perhaps, knew what it was to have a passionate yearning for the Truth as Truth, who never made a sacrifice in the search, or for the maintenance, of it, and never, in fact, gave himself an hour's hard ' thinking ' in his life? " And he went on to quote a case where free inquiry had cost a clergyman £9,000.

The difficulty was a peculiarly Anglican one. How could one, either in logic or in practice, effectively sponsor private judgment as against Rome, and at the same time impose authority against free thought and individualistic Protestantism?

Colenso indeed, had been directly charged with dishonesty in retaining his bishopric. The *Guardian*, for instance, had said (3rd Dec., 1862): " It is high time that amiable and conscientious persons such as he is, cease to deceive themselves by the shallow talk with which he closes his preface about the Church ' representing the religious life of the nation ' and ' requiring to protest against all perversions of the truth, etc.' The Church of England is a religious society which takes pledges as to the tenets of her office bearers before she commissions them. In truth no religious society can be carried on at all except on some such plan as this. It is not open to an honourable man to accept her places of influence and dignity and then to employ these advantages in abandoning the very principles on which she is founded."

To this kind of accusation and Tait's statement that a man who came to disbelieve the Church's doctrines, " of course would resign his office as one of the Church's authorised teachers," Colenso had a reply ready: " Wycliffe did not retire from his sacred office, though disbelieving the doctrines of the Church of which he was a minister, and that Cranmer, Ridley, and Latimer, and other Bishops, although consecrated as bishops of the Roman Church, and bound by the solemn vows of their ordination in that Church, did not *resign* their sees as soon as they became *Protestant* bishops."

This point was very hard to answer. It brought Colenso's opponents face to face with the fact, which they had preferred to forget, that the Church of England had once contained, and still implicitly contained, a revolutionary element which authority would find it hard to crush.

Again, Colenso was able to show that it was partly chance that had brought him into disrepute as a heretic. No clergyman completely fulfilled the law in liturgical matters; no one was punished for neglecting the theoretically binding obligation to recite the Athanasian creed in public. An unknown number of clergy, but certainly many, had a doctrinal position as dubiously reconcilable with the formularies as Colenso's own. He was able to point to a statement of Longley, Archbishop of Canterbury, to the effect that the Archbishop would rather go to prison than pronounce the words of the Burial Service in certain cases. An individualistic church was a dangerous place in which to begin throwing the stones of authority.

It is difficult to tell how far Colenso gradually came to diverge in doctrine from the bulk of his fellow Anglicans.

His mind was so dominated by a few grand and simple religious ideas—the greatness and goodness of God, the brotherhood of the human race, the binding authority of conscience. No doubt he believed more than this, but these seem to have been the only doctrines that he found imaginatively important and inspiring; and it was of these that he constantly wrote. He never defined his theological position in full, for when his voluminous writings are not dealing with these basic ideas, they invariably turn to the minutiæ of Biblical criticism. One has the impression—it is hardly more—that as time went on he attached less and less importance to the creeds, the sacraments, and the Anglican liturgy, and that his dissatisfaction with what he considered the spiritual blindness of his Church constantly grew.

But it must not be supposed that all the conscious orthodoxy was on Gray's side; there was still the crucial question of the Royal supremacy. It was natural that Colenso, repudiated by his fellow bishops, should look to the Crown and the courts to vindicate him. On the Royal supremacy he based his counter attack. In his *Remarks on the Proceedings of the Bishop of Cape Town* (1864) Colenso issued this challenge to Gray: " Either you will leave it [the question of Colenso's orthodoxy] to the Queen, or reject the Queen's supremacy." In Colenso's eyes it was Gray who was the heretic and the innovator, by the very fact that he claimed a doctrinal jurisdiction independent of the Crown. It was battle between rigid doctrine and the power of the bishops on one side and private judgment and the Royal supremacy on the other.

But the Royal supremacy as a doctrine was one thing; the practical working of the doctrine in the decisions of Her Majesty's courts was a different and more elusive one. No one at any time in the Victorian period was able to predict with certainty how the courts would decide an ecclesiastical case. But the decision in *Essays and Reviews* seemed to many a definite, and as it ultimately proved, an accurate pointer. The courts were taking a Broad Church, anti-dogmatic anti-episcopal line. Colenso wrote jubilantly, if not quite accurately, in a letter of 29th March, 1864, that the " judgment sweeps away at a stroke the whole farrago of the Bishop of Cape Town's judgment." He was right to this extent: the Privy Council would indeed reverse Gray's judgment on Colenso, but for both prelates there were still surprises in store.

V

If the feeling of outraged orthodoxy was common to both Gray and Colenso, so was the feeling of being persecuted. It may have seemed obvious to Colenso and to the majority of the British public that Colenso was the persecuted one, and this brought him the great advantage of wide popular support. To Gray it seemed very different; when he examined the letters patent from the Crown, this is what he found: " In case any proceedings shall be instituted against any of the said Bishops of Grahamstown and Natal . . . such proceedings shall originate and be carried on before the said Bishop of Cape Town, whom we hereby authorise and direct to take cognisance of the same." Gray may have been rather apt to imagine agreement with himself in persons who really differed. But he can surely be excused for think-ing, in view of these words, and of the widespread doubt which was certainly felt about Colenso's orthodoxy, that it was his duty alike to the Church and to the Crown to sit in judgment upon him. Accordingly the case was brought and Colenso was convicted of heresy. An appeal was lodged, and eventually the case came before the Judicial Committee of the Privy Council.

It is not necessary to go into the details of the arguments that were presented. The proceedings make a sad spectacle. Colenso and Gray had always been at cross-purposes during the controversy. They did not speak the same theological language; but each in his different way had the religious issues profoundly at heart. Each was a devoted missionary; each had sacrificed for his faith an easy life among friends and familiar things in England—an unspectacular sacrifice, perhaps, but one which strikes daily at the heart over long years. The courage of each might, if it had been required, have reached up to the ordeal of martyrdom. Now a third incommensurable, a legal decision, entered the story to the further confusion of these already perplexed men. It cut right across the religious issues; it ignored them utterly.

The judgment of the Judicial Committee of the Privy Council, 20th March, 1865, was lengthy as such documents are. But it contained a sentence which shattered the assumptions upon which each side had acted, "The Crown (it said) had no power to constitute a bishopric in a colony which has its own independent legislature." It followed from this that the authority given by the Crown to the Bishop of Cape Town over the Bishop of Natal was void, and therefore that Gray's sentence on Colenso was void. The effect of this judgment was well-summarised by the *Guardian*: " This bishop . . . now turns out after all to be a mockery and a sham; to have no diocese, to have no patent except one which is absolutely ' null and void'; and to be in fact, as far as the law of England goes, if a bishop at all, at least a bishop of nothing. This in effect, says Lord Westbury's judgment, is the real result of all that has been done in this department for the last twenty years."

In effect, the Crown in the person of its judges proclaimed

itself to have no authority and, on the basis of this lack of authority, interfered decisively with the spiritual affairs of the South African Church. A year or two before the Privy Council's decision, Bishop Gray had wished, for very adequate moral reasons, to deprive a clergyman of his preferment. His decision to deprive was upheld in the South African courts. As we have by now come to expect in ecclesiastical cases, the decision was reversed by higher authority. When the case was brought to London, the courts declared that the synod that Bishop Gray had called was illegal, and that his sentence of deprivation was void.

After these two contrasting experiences of the law, operating at its highest level, and speaking with its most solemn voice, Gray had reason to feel perplexed, and to wonder whether after all he himself and not his subordinate was in reality the persecuted one. The law apparently would neither allow the South African Church to run its own affairs, because this was damaging to the authority of the Crown, nor would it endorse the authority which the Crown had bestowed in perfectly plain language upon Gray as Bishop of Cape Town. The Crown apparently had not enough power to act in South Africa, in ecclesiastical matters; it could not delegate authority, but it had just enough authority to make it impious and disloyal for the bishops to make any decisions of their own. The Crown would not act; it would only apparently interfere to prevent anything from being done. Is it any wonder that Gray felt that he was persecuted?

It was certainly a puzzling and even an ambiguous judgment; and Gray's feeling about it gradually changed. If he still felt ill-treated, he nevertheless came to see a brighter side to the affair. Tactically, no doubt, it was a victory for Colenso and a defeat for Gray. But beyond that several interpretations were possible. Gray's judgment on Colenso had been nullified, and Colenso's oath of obedience to Gray had been held to be of no account.

But another side to the question was expressed by Gray in a letter which he wrote to his son 9th May, 1865: "Intending to destroy the power of bishops, the Lord Chancellor bids fair to exalt it." Pusey, who of course supported Gray throughout, also welcomed the judgment as freeing the African Church from the power of the State. If the Crown claims no jurisdiction, so ran the argument, the Church must become a voluntary body, and then the spiritual authority of the bishops, backed by voluntary oaths of obedience promised by the clergy, would be supreme, as it had been in the early Church before Christianity became official. So Gray and his friends were left, not sure whether they were to rejoice or to mourn.

For Colenso the Privy Council's decision was equally puzzling. He had been reinstated as far as the power of the State could do it. But doctrinally the judgment went dead against his convictions. The Church of England, in his view, could only rest on the Royal supremacy. If the Crown itself renounced or denied this supremacy, Colenso was reduced either to believing that the Crown really possessed an authority which it irrevocably refused to exercise—a position intellectually dubious and practically quite hopeless—or to saying that the South African Church was an entirely independent body. In the second case it was hard to see how he could in logic repudiate the ecclesiastical superior to whom he had sworn obedience. Colenso, in fact, was left without any consistent principle of Church government.

V I

Colenso had seen a favourable omen in the decision of the Privy Council on *Essays and Reviews*. There were others who also saw a close connection between the two cases, but found the connection a very menacing one. On 9th February, 1863, 41 bishops gathered together in England (Thirlwall was the only dissentient) had issued a remonstrance to Colenso which balanced stern warning with courtesy. It said, in part: " Now it cannot have escaped you that the inconsistency between the office you hold and the opinions you avow is causing great pain and grievous scandal to the Church. And we solemnly ask you to consider once more, with the most serious attention, whether you can, without harm to your own conscience, retain your position, when you can no longer discharge its duties or use the formularies to which you have subscribed. We will not abandon the hope, that, through earnest prayer and deeper study of God's Word, you may, under the guidance of the Holy Spirit, be restored to a state of belief in which you may be able with a clear conscience again to discharge the duties of our sacred office; a result which, from regard to your highest interests, we should welcome with the most unfeigned satisfaction. We are, your faithful brethren in Christ."

This is the language of confident men, who believed themselves to be in command of events. The question seemed at this point to be, " Would Colenso resign, or would he recant? " But just a year later (the affair moved slowly because of the great distances and the judicial heights which it involved), the judgment on *Essays and Reviews* cast a new and for the English bishops sinister light on the affair. They no longer felt sure that, being 41 bishops against one,

they had ample reserves of strength for any conflict with
Colenso. If the courts could accept *Essays and Reviews* as
sound Anglican doctrine, they might also come to accept
Colenso on the Pentateuch. The *Essays and Reviews* decision
made both sides fiercer. It made Colenso more confident of
success; and it made the orthodox more frightened of dam-
age to the faith from a series of irresponsible, time-serving
legal decisions, which might whittle away every essential
doctrine, and lead in the end to complete religious indif-
ferentism. And so, when the bishops considered the matter
again after the *Essays and Reviews* decision, their mood was
widely different. How did it come about that Anglican
bishops, normally the most law-abiding of men, decided
to consecrate a bishop in the teeth of the power of the
State and the declared decision of the courts? We must
now examine the events that led to this unexampled climax.

First, the Privy Council decision of 20th March, 1865,
which has already been outlined, brought it home to all
who cared for any traditional kind of Anglicanism whether
High Church or Low Church, that the decision in *Essays and
Reviews* had been no isolated or accidental case. It seemed
that there was now a settled policy on the part of the courts
to prevent the enforcement upon the clergy of any standards
of belief. In the eyes of the bishops the doctrinal oath of
the clergy had by now been deprived, as far as secular law
was concerned, of all its meaning and value. They almost
felt that there was no guarantee that an atheist might not
soon be nominated as a bishop. The difference between the
moderate attitude of the bishops in 1863 and their determined defiance of the State a few years later can be paralleled perhaps by the movement of British opinion about
German aggression between 1938 and 1940. A moderate
and distant threat made them timid, a close and immeasur-
able one made them reckless.

The second major cause of the bishops' decision to appoint a new bishop as rival to Colenso was to be found paradoxically in the gradual realisation that the doctrinal case against Colenso was not so strong as it looked. As long as they had been sure that, according to the plain language of Prayer Book and Articles, Colenso was heretical, the English bishops had felt comparatively tolerant, though always of course disapproving. They could regard his book as a sad but isolated aberration. No one, they felt, could imagine that a man had any possible right to combine such subversive opinions with the enjoyment of a bishopric. The Privy Council had dealt one blow to this assumption. Dean Stanley was now to deal another.

Three months after the Privy Council's decision, a motion was placed before the Lower House of Convocation expressing admiration for the South African bishops, that is to say, for Gray and his associates in the work of denouncing and deposing Colenso. On 28th June, 1865, Stanley made a momentous speech upon this motion; what he said put the whole question in a new light. It must be remembered that Stanley was more than an ordinary dean. He was not merely a very famous Churchman, the biographer of Arnold, the intimate friend of the Queen. His voice had, to the British public at large, an unmistakably official ring. No ecclesiastical cause that he supported could be regarded as certainly lost; if he supported Colenso, Colenso must be much more than a solitary fanatic. But it was not so much the fact of Stanley's support for Colenso, which could perhaps have been foreseen, as his arguments which made a really profound impression. "Am I to understand," he asked, "that this House has made up its mind on the question that it is unlawful for a clergyman, a prelate of the Church of England, to deny the Mosaic origin of any portion of the Pentateuch? I wish the House to consider whether that is the position we take up—that to question any portion of the Mosaic origin of the Pentateuch, in our judgment, excludes anyone from holding any office in the Church of England. Again, we mean also, by concurring in this Address, to declare that we have made up our minds that it is unlawful for any clergyman of the Church of England to hold the opinion concerning future punishment which was held by Origen and by St. Gregory of Nyssa, and that any person who holds such opinion cannot hold any office within the Church of England. Again, we are called upon to assert that we have made up our minds that any person who holds the views on the Atonement that were held by Alexander Knox, that were held by William Law, that were held by Coleridge, that were held by St. Anselm and by St. Chrysostom, may not hold any office in the Church of England."

Here Stanley was meeting Gray upon his own ground. Gray had appealed, not so much to the formularies of the Church of England as to the undivided Church, the traditional Christianity of the first thousand years. Colenso and his supporters, because on the whole they cared little for the early Church, had allowed this part of the argument to go by default. Colenso simply replied that he was not bound to believe what the early Church believed. But now Stanley's searching query dramatically opened this part of the argument. Could one after all be certain that Gray's interpretation of Biblical inspiration was the traditional one? Here of course, though his purpose was to defend him, Stanley disagreed also with Colenso. Gray and Colenso agreed that the Old Testament was history, though Gray thought it good history and Colenso thought it bad. As often happens in a dispute, the point agreed without discussion was really the most open to question; Stanley was the first to put his finger on it.

But Stanley's next point was more searching still. "I might mention one who, although on some of these awful and mysterious questions he has expressed no direct opinion, yet has ventured to say that the Pentateuch is not the work of Moses; who has ventured to say that there are parts of the Sacred Scriptures which are poetical and not historical; who has ventured to say that the Holy Scriptures themselves rise infinitely by our being able to acknowledge both that poetical character and also the historical incidents in their true historical reality; who has ventured to say that the narratives of those historical incidents are coloured, not unfrequently, by the necessary infirmities which belong to the human instruments by which they are conveyed—and that individual is the one who now addresses you. I am not unwilling to take my place with Gregory of Nyssa, with Jerome, and with Athanasius. But in that same goodly company I shall find the despised and rejected Bishop of Natal. At least deal out the same measure to me that you deal to him; at least judge for all a righteous judgment."

Stanley was here drawing attention to the curious, random operation of Anglican discipline. No one had seriously thought of indicting Stanley for heresy. But if Colenso was guilty according to law, so too was Stanley, a respected leader of the powerful Broad Church party. If he was guilty, how many others, living unmolested and contented, must be guilty likewise?

And in any case, what constituted guilt? The Articles said: "Holy Scripture containeth all things necessary to salvation." This Colenso (and Stanley) had never denied. The courts had ruled that Colenso had nowhere in his writings contravened this statement. Now the Articles had been written before Biblical criticism began; when the issue that troubled men's minds was not the truth of the Bible but its interpretation. In the sixteenth century people had desired an answer to the questions, should the Bible be interpreted by Church or by individual, and, ought it to be the servant or the master of the Church's teaching? So this sixteenth century formula was quite unequipped to deal with the unimaginable errors of the nineteenth. The men who drew it up, assuming it to be agreed that the Bible was true, had not troubled to define in what sense or within what limits it must be regarded as true. Yet these sixteenth century formulas were for the courts the sole standard of judgment. When written laws do not cover the case in dispute, judges inevitably become the creators instead of the interpreters of law.

Considerations such as these, fortified by bitter experience of legal decisions in practice, forced the bishops to recognise that some more decisive, more contemporary exercise of authority was needed. The Articles had been framed to elucidate doctrinal differences between churches. A new technique was needed to deal with controversies that might strike at the root of the Christian faith.

Some twenty years before, W. G. Ward had said that the Thirty-Nine Articles were consistent with every defined doctrine of the Church of Rome. The universal astonishment which had greeted this remark had by now faded. Ward had long left the Church of England, and Newman, whose Tract XC had been devoted to a subtle justification of Ward's proposition, had departed also. Now the new and opposite, but essentially similar, claim was being made, that the Articles were consistent with the rejection of almost all dogmatic belief. The similarity lay in this: that in each case partisans were appealing, not to the general sense of the Articles (which had so easily satisfied devotees of Church and King in earlier generations), but to their minimum legal and literal meaning. Ward wished to believe more and Colenso less than the framers of the Articles seemed to intend.

Ward wished to empty the negative, anti-Roman phrases of their meaning; Colenso wished to nullify much of the positive doctrinal content. In this process of these two searching examinations it became clear that the Articles could mean an infinite number of different things. Nothing was more certain on grounds of history and commonsense than that the Articles did not intend to admit the whole of Roman doctrine; it was almost equally clear that they did not intend the Latitudinarianism of Colenso or of some of the authors of *Essays and Reviews*. But in a lawyer's eyes (and the bishops trembled as they recalled that only through lawyer's eyes could the Privy Council consider the affair) the Articles might admit of both interpretations, and of countless others.

But the great difference between the maximalist inter-pretation of the forties and the minimalist one of the sixties was that Ward and Newman had had no backing from the courts or the Crown. Moreover, they had soon ceased to adhere to the English Church, and had therefore abandoned the attempt to reconcile the Articles with their own beliefs. At the same time those of their allies that remained, Pusey and the rest, had been placed permanently on the defensive. But Colenso and his hidden, and doubtless large collection of sympathisers, had no intention of abandoning the Church. They desired rather to alter it to fit their purpose.

VII

So it came about that the bishops were no longer what they had been in 1863, a group of men calmly and reasonably pointing out to Colenso the clear terms of the agreed doctrinal formulas which he had flouted; they had become some four years later anxious men working vehemently as if to plug gaps in a dyke. Stanley's brilliant advocacy had done much to bring about the change because it clearly represented a widely held opinion. There was one point in particular in Stanley's indictment which they could not meet. Why was doctrinal discipline in the Church so arbitrary? Why should Colenso be punished and Stanley go free? The bishops were not to blame for the anomaly, for they had no power to expand or to develop the sixteenth century formulas. Thus there could be no valid test of orthodoxy laid down in black and white. As long as a man avoided the heresies which had agitated the framers of the Articles (often an easy task for the most unorthodox) it seemed that there were no legal restrictions upon the expression of his views.

And so the bishops, unable to appeal to any satisfactory documents, convinced that the courts were a broken reed, felt that they had to strike out to make an example to assert their authority. To many of the bishops, to Gray and Wilberforce especially, the alternative seemed to be either firm action now against Colenso as the foremost representative of multifarious errors, or general chaos and the disintegration of the Church. So it happened that Gray, whose temperamental and doctrinal rigidity was far from typical of the bench of bishops, was able to sweep away for the moment their love of compromise and their traditional acceptance of State control, and to persuade them to a memorable act of defiance. But this was not to be achieved without much heart-searching.

The Dean of Pietermaritzburg had written from Africa to Archbishop Longley of Canterbury to ask whether the acceptance of the new bishop in Colenso's place by the clergy and laity of Natal would cut them off from the Anglican communion. A straight and simple question, but not so easy to answer.

It was partly in order to answer it that the first Lambeth conference was summoned by Archbishop Longley. Longley was a cautious man and from the outset he made it clear that the conference's authority and scope would both be limited. Nevertheless, the idea of a conference of Anglican bishops from the whole English-speaking world introduced a disturbing element. The English Church had for so long depended upon custom rather than strict principle to determine its relations with the State. Custom is only a satisfactory guide if everyone concerned has a similar background of thought. Both Gray and Colenso were English by birth and education. But American bishops could not be expected to feel any great awe for the law of England and the prerogatives of the Crown. Their very presence made a decisive repudiation of State authority more probable.

Bishop Tait's diary allows us to appreciate the lingering doubts with which many of the bishops, met together at Lambeth, received the daring proposals of Gray and his friends: " The Bishop of Cape Town suddenly proposed that the conference should adopt the resolution of Convocation respecting Natal [i.e. to consecrate a new bishop in place of Colenso]. The greatest confusion ensued. He declared that he would resign his bishopric unless his proposal was adopted. No one knew what the resolution which he proposed we should adopt was. It was with great difficulty that we could get what he wanted read. I got from him the Chronicle of Convocation, from which he was reading, and found that he had omitted the first clause of a hypothetical sentence—' *If* it be decided that a new Bishop for Natal should be consecrated.' I insisted on these words being inserted. A vote was hurried on, and began to be taken. The Bishop of Winchester moved that the subject be referred to the committee on the Natal question. Cape Town's friends became greatly excited. Oxford protested that the question had been put, and that it was not competent now to introduce an amendment. Cape Town tried to get both the resolutions passed by Convocation adopted by us. The Archbishop (who ought, after his previous decision, to have prevented this new question from being raised at the last moment) thought that the Bishop of Winchester's amendment was too late and could not be put. I besought them not to carry so important a resolution by a ' ruse,' but in vain.

" Then Gloucester (our admirable secretary) insisted that the one resolution only, viz, the hypothetical one, should be put. It was put, and carried almost unanimously."

The bishops must have felt during all this that a decisive step was imminent. But mid-Victorian religious history is a series of false summits. Gauntlets are thrown down; irrevocable decisions are made; the courts expound the law once and for all. But as a rule there are second thoughts, hesitations, and changed decisions in reserve. So it was here, for the resolution only said, " if it be decided that a new bishop should be consecrated." Tait confided to his diary that, after all, no great harm had been done. Gray's first effort to depose and replace Colenso had after all been thwarted.

But Gray was a very determined man. He demanded a new bishop, not merely to administer the diocese of Natal, but to blot out a terrible disgrace. He had already, as he thought, found the right man, William Butler, then Vicar of Wantage, later to be Dean of Lincoln. But Butler eventually, after receiving a letter from Tait explaining the dangers that would lie in the appointment of a man of marked opinions, declined the task. Other men were canvassed unsuccessfully, and at last the choice fell upon an Accrington vicar, W. K. Macrorie. Clearly the new bishop could not have a mandate from the Crown, for Colenso continued to possess this. To consecrate a bishop without that mandate would have been, a few years earlier, an act unimaginable to most of the bishops. Now they braced themselves for it with many inward misgivings. A symbol of their general uncertainty is to be seen perhaps in the difficulty they found in agreeing upon a place for consecration. Bishop Tait, who was regarded as the man most likely to prevent anything from being done, received a stream of confidential letters, giving a series of times and places for the proposed consecration. In letters varying from the tone of wartime dispatches of a spy from the enemy capital, to that of a man giving a racing tip, now Oxford was mentioned, now Wantage, and now Edinburgh. Even Gray and Wilberforce, determined as they were, were not quite certain that they could take full responsibility for the momentous act, and the responsibility for it was freely bandied about. The project, at first tentatively supported by Archbishop Longley, to consecrate in his province of Canterbury was discarded in favour of Scotland. But the Scottish bishops, warned as usual by Tait of the risks they might run, at length rejected the burden. Indeed, men found it hard to say whether their doubts and hesitation were really dictated by worldly fears or by the voice of conscience. The Secretary of State for the Colonies issued this warning: " Her Majesty's Government look upon this intention [consecration of a new bishop] with apprehension and regret. . . . If after being warned of the views of Her Majesty's Government, any ecclesiastical officer holding a *salaried*[1] office during the pleasure of Her Majesty were to be a party to any such transaction, Her Majesty's Government would consider it their duty to advise the Queen to cancel his appointment." But though discretion showed the danger of consecrating Macrorie in England, the bishops

[1]My italics

116

could point to the Privy Council decision that the Queen's ecclesiastical writ did not run in South Africa. It was this decision that had once nullified the legal effect of Gray's judgment on Colenso. The same decision could now be used to nullify the government's desire to prevent Gray from carrying out his plan. In this instance Erastianism made very high claims for the State machine, only to find them defeated by the working of that same machine. So Britain never witnessed the much-discussed consecration; but when it took place in Cape Town cathedral the government did not interfere. This took place after a long delay early in 1869. It is recorded by Mr. La Touche, one of the clergy who supported and helped Colenso, that when Colenso and Macrorie met in the streets of their African diocese, Colenso would make a conventional greeting, which Macrorie considered it his duty to ignore. Two rival bishops faced each other, each consecrated to the forms of the Church of England, each claiming to be the only true Anglican representative. Each, too, must have been puzzled, for there seemed to be no answer to the dilemma posed by their rivalry. To what authority could they appeal? Crown, courts, episcopate had already given their verdict, and the deadlock remained. The affair settled down to an uneasy equilibrium.

Colenso retained a devoted band of followers, but it was a personal following only, and therefore a small and dwindling one. He remained a famous name, and when he visited England he was something of a lion at London dinner-parties. But neither the British nor the South African Government intervened to help him. His position as the bishop recognised by the Crown entailed no practical advantages for the future. Macrorie was accepted as the legitimate bishop by all the other South African bishops, and by the bulk of the laity of Natal. Colenso remained at his post. Anthony Trollope who heard him preach in 1878 reported that the church was "not crowded but by no means deserted." As his faithful followers disappeared, they were seldom replaced by young recruits. He consecrated no new bishop; and when he died in 1883, his small group of followers were without a bishop for over seventy years. It was not until the 1950's that they persuaded a bishop of Anglican consecration, who had left the Anglican communion, to come and rule over them.[1] By this time it had long been clear that the practical victory lay with Macrorie and his successors.

VIII

The case had ended dramatically, and had posed searching and unanswered questions for all who cared for the theoretical basis of the Church of England. What next? Was the uneasy marriage of Church and State finally dissolved? Anglicans, for the most part, cared more for the practical working of their Church than for its theoretical justification. People were slow, deliberately slow, perhaps wisely slow, to see the implications of the affair. No one thought of having two rival Bishops of Lichfield. South Africa was a long way away; in the fullness of time no doubt Colenso would disappear. The leaders of Church and State thought of other things. The bishops began to consider their attitude to the approaching Vatican Council. By many the unanswered questions were eagerly forgotten.

Colenso and Gray were left like orators each in a separate deserted hall. Each in his own way had a powerful case; each had a firm hold on half the Anglican tradition. Were these two traditions now separate? Were they to be un-

[1]See note at end.

twined for good? Was the work of three centuries useless
to maintain unity? But gradually passion subsided in
Africa as it had in England. Both Colenso and Gray were
by nature just and generous men. When Gray died, Colenso
preached in Natal cathedral on 22nd September, 1872, a
remarkable sermon. He said that Gray had had one single
object mainly in view. " To advance what he deemed the
cause most dear to God and most beneficial to man; and that
in labours for this end, most unselfish and unwearied, in
season and out of season, with energy which beat down all
obstructions, with courage that faced all opposition, with
faith which laid firmly hold of the Unseen Hand, he spent
and was spent, body and soul in His service. To him we
owe it that the foundations of the life of the Church of
England were laid in this diocese. . . . For myself I remember
that he was once my friend and my father, and that we took
sweet counsel together; and the fact that since then he has
felt it to be his duty to censure and condemn my proceedings has only added special solemnity to this event which has
removed him into a sphere where even now he beholds the
truth in the clear shining of God's light."

Dean Stanley, speaking in Convocation shortly after-
wards, read out part of Colenso's sermon and said: " It is
a testimony creditable alike to the Bishop of Cape Town,
who could inspire such sentiments, and to the Bishop of
Natal who gave utterance to them. And when he, the first
missionary bishop of Africa, who translated the Holy
Scriptures into the language of the natives (Colenso), shall
be called to his rest, I trust that there will be found some
prelate presiding over the see of Cape Town just and generous
enough to render the like honour to the Bishop of Natal."

If this hope was not literally fulfilled, its spirit was reflected
in the pronouncement of Green, Dean of Pietermaritzburg,
who had been ineffectually declared deposed from his

position by Colenso, just as Colenso had been ineffectually declared deposed by Gray. When Colenso died in 1883, Green said in a sermon: " A month ago I had occasion to write to him; he replied in terms of very warm regard, saying in respect of something I had written, ' which act of charity may God return tenfold into your bosom.' May this prayer for me, whom men might think he could not feel kindly towards, be returned a hundredfold to him." And so the *odium theologicum* was splendidly buried.

CHAPTER SIX

Conclusion

BUT LONG after the high passions of the Colenso affair had been calmed and when memories even had grown dim, the abiding importance of the affair remained, reaching out into the twentieth century. For the bishops of the Church of England had successfully defied the State. On every previous occasion in the nineteenth century, when the interests of Church and State seemed to clash, they had achieved nothing more than fruitless protest. We have seen what happened only a few years before in the case of *Essays and Reviews*. The Colenso case was a landmark because it showed unequivocally that bishops, in spite of the manner of their appointment, did not regard themselves as a department of State. They did not concur with Matthew Arnold (and one might add perhaps Henry VIII) who held that the Church was the State in its religious aspect. This was more important than the rights of the dispute between Colenso and Gray.

Implicit in the Thirty-Nine Articles, and in the whole sixteenth century settlement, had lain the question, if the Church's faith is this, and the King is the supreme governor, what happens if the King directs the Church to think otherwise? The bishops, rightly or wrongly, saw in the decision of the courts about Colenso an attempt to change the Church's faith. Against this the bishops set up their own conception of spiritual liberty, designed as it were to take the place of their fast-disappearing material advantages.

But this new conception was only achieved at the price of rejecting a zealous bishop and causing him to appear in the eyes of many as a martyr.

So the bishops emerged with enhanced prestige from the affair. All churches have doctrinal crises and disputes about authority; this one seemed to have died down as quietly as most. To those who judge the machinery of a church's government by standards which might apply to a council or a club, it may have seemed that not very much was amiss. But there are always some who are interested, not in the practical working of a church but in its theoretical justification. There are those who want a clear answer to awkward questions, and who desire more than any particular doctrine, a voice, " as of one having authority and not as the scribes."

To such persons the Colenso case, like the two previous ones which we have discussed, presented a host of unanswered questions. What disciplinary action could be taken against a bishop, and by whom? Had the Archbishop of Canterbury authority over bishops, or was he *primus inter pares?* If the sentence of a metropolitan, judging another bishop, were not binding, to whom did an appeal lie? Had the whole body of bishops any power over one of their number? Who in the last resort was master, the bishops or the King?

To such enquiring minds the proceedings seemed equally unsatisfactory, whether they regarded Colenso as guilty or innocent. If he were guilty, the courts had rendered his guilt unpunishable. If he were innocent, he had been condemned unheard by the bench of bishops. Indeed there was no established procedure by which they could hear him and deal judicially with charges against him. Their condemnation, right or wrong, was a shot in the dark.

And behind all these unanswered questions yet larger questions loomed. Now that experience had shown beyond question that the Thirty-Nine Articles were not in the nineteenth century an effective test of faith—because they were indecisive, denied more than they affirmed, and entirely ignored those questions which most deeply agitated nineteenth century thought—what rule of faith was there? If the bishops were to be independent of the State they must have a principle on which to base their resistance. When they appealed to the Church's teaching, what did they mean?

One of the great divisions between thinking people of the time lay between those who regarded such questions as unimportant, or better left to each man to answer for himself, and those who demanded firm answers, and often, not receiving them, abandoned the Church of England. To many, whether they left the Church before or after the Colenso case, this demand was crucial. It was a demand which linked the most diverse intellectual positions. It was a demand common to Manning and Huxley.

Note

THE ARCHBISHOP of Canterbury, Dr. Fisher, said in a statement issued yesterday that unless the Rt. Rev. G. F. B. Morris withdrew from the position of Bishop of the Church of England in South Africa, " I must regard him as having put himself out of Communion with the See of Canterbury and outside the fellowship of the Anglican Communion."

The statement also said: " In order to avoid misunderstandings which may arise from the announcement that a small body known as The Church of England in South Africa has elected the Rt. Rev. G. F. B. Morris to be its bishop, I must make clear that this body has no place in the constitutional system of the Church of England and is not amenable to the jurisdiction of the Archbishop of Canterbury.

" Bishop Morris has accepted episcopal office in this body against the advice and direction of the Archbishop of Canterbury and without any reference to the Archbishop of Cape Town. He has thus acted against the principles of Church Order observed in the Anglican Communion."

A reply authorised by Bishop Morris was issued in London later by the Rev. F. W. Martin, of Great Horkesley Rectory, Colchester, and the Rev. P. E. Hughes. It refers to the Church of the Province of South Africa, which, Bishop Morris says, is a schismatic church, and states: " The Archbishops of Canterbury and York condemned the schismatic

Church founded by Bishop Gray in 1870: this Church is now called the Church of the Province of South Africa. The Church of England in South Africa has adhered to the Book of Common Prayer with the Thirty-Nine Articles and is recognised by the Government of South Africa, a sovereign, independent State of the Commonwealth.

" The truth is that in South Africa the Church of England is recognised by Government departments and is registered as such.

" There are scores of African congregations which have remained true to our Protestant Evangelical faith, together with some powerful European Churches. These have all been denied the ministration of a bishop of their own, up to the present time.

" No good purpose can be served by seeking to discredit the Church of England in South Africa or by threatening to expel me from communion with the See of Canterbury. It is a form of persecution which will bring discredit on those who practise it. There can be no agreement or concordat with the Church of the Province which has deliberately eliminated the Thirty-Nine Articles, promotes such a manual as *The Mass our Sacrifice*, advises the invocation of the Saints, prayers for the dead, and other pro-Roman practices."

Bishop Morris was bishop in North Africa from 1943 to 1954. He retired from the position last November and later accepted an invitation to act as rector of Christ Church, Hillbrow. By unanimous vote last month the annual synod of the Church of England in South Africa elected him to be Bishop.

INDEX

NOTE. *All dates given in brackets are dates of birth*